DEEPER

Finding the Depth Dimension
Beneath the Surface of Life

DEEPER

Finding the Depth Dimension
Beneath the Surface of Life

SHARON GRUSSENDORFF

Anamchara Books
Vestal, NY 13850
www.anamcharabooks.com

Print ISBN: 978-1-62524-844-2
eBook ISBN: 978-1-62524-845-9

CONTENTS

ACKNOWLEDGMENTS

I have had the privilege of participating in the Center for Action and Contemplation's Living School from 2015 to 2017. This book emerged out of the richness I have gained from the teachings of Richard Rohr, James Finley, and Cynthia Bourgeault, and the profound inner process they facilitated during my time in the Living School. I also wish to express my gratitude to my fellow students in the Living School, particularly those in my circle group, who have journeyed with me in this transformative process.

I would also like to give special thanks to the members (past and present) of the Dove Fellowship and all who support the Solitude Retreat Centre, for traveling with me on this contemplative journey.

I am praying again, Awesome One. . . .
I yearn to be held
in the great hands of your heart—
oh let them take me now.
Into them I place these fragments, my life,
and you, God—spend them however you want.

—RAINER MARIA RILKE

INTRODUCTION

The first time I got into a pool when I was small, I was too scared to venture away from the edge. I clutched the side with white knuckles, slowly inching my way around the pool but never letting go. Someone called to me, "You will have more fun if you let go of the side of the pool." The thought terrified me, but I gradually eased my grip, testing the water briefly at first and then for longer periods, until eventually I was floating in the middle of the pool. The feeling of freedom and joy as I lay back looking up at a vast blue sky, held by the cool water, was a beautiful discovery.

This memory came back to me many years later on a silent retreat. I was tentatively exploring a practice of contemplative prayer, but I struggled with the idea of letting go of my familiar sense of relating with God in relaxed and open conversational prayer. While grapping with this, the phrase flashed across my mind: "Let go of the side of the pool."

As a child, I had wanted to limit myself to the known, safe way of being in the pool—only to discover a sense of greater freedom when I finally let go of the edge. The invitation to me now was to let go of my mind's images and constructs, including my known way of connecting with God, and dare to float freely into the mystery and holding love of God. This invitation to let go required a loss of control and certainty, but without this loss, I knew I would never experience the wild and exhilarating freedom that comes from complete abandonment to God.

This book is an invitation to explore the freedom and joy that is possible when we allow ourselves to float freely in the love of God—when we let go of the safe edges of our spirituality so we can experience the delicious release and freedom of entrusting ourselves to God's expansive embrace. Letting go of our minds' certainty (and with that our usual ways of knowing and connecting with God) can feel frightening at first, because we are so used to the way of knowing with which we grew up. But just as a child will never learn to trust the water's buoyancy until she releases her grip on the side of the pool, so we will never learn how safely and tenderly we are held in God if we do not let go of our ideas about what God's love looks like or feels like. We have to venture away from the known to experience the unknown. We have to let go of *ideas about* God and love to *experience* these directly for ourselves.

The analogy of letting go of the side of the pool is a fairly simple one, but I have found it a very useful image for my own contemplative journey. It illustrates the enormous shift that has to take place in our spiritual lives—the shift from control to surrender, from the effort of clinging to the release of resting, from anxiously saving our own lives to trusting Another to hold us.

Letting go of the side of the pool is both a mental gesture in the moment and a long-term process of gradually allowing the grip of the mind to ease on all the multiple layers of identity and security we have built up over the years. In this book, we will explore some of the ways in which we can recognize and participate with this on-going process of inner transformation.

PART I

The Invitation
to a Deeper Journey

1

The Inner Freedom
of the Depth Dimension

Why do I spend so much of my life trapped like this,
on the outer circumference
of the inner richness of my own life?
Why do I spend so much time unaware
of that which alone can fulfil my heart?

—JAMES FINLEY[1]

James Finley asks a very important question: Why do we settle for such a superficial existence and miss out on the depth and inner richness that is possible?

I once heard Finley describe the depth dimension of life using the analogy of a multidimensional timeline. The period of time from our births to our deaths—our chronological lives, with all the events we experience along the way—is plotted on the horizontal dimension of the timeline. At each moment on this horizontal line, there is also a depth dimension. This is the dimension in which we know our abiding union with God. Our capacity to experience this is infinitely deep, but the depth dimension can only be accessed in the present moment.

Degrees of Freedom

Physics has a wonderful term called "degrees of freedom." An object that is free to move in one dimension has one degree of freedom; it can move back and forth in a straight line, but this is all it can do. If an object can move in two dimensions, for example, in any direction on a flat page, it has two degrees of freedom. Our physical bodies have three degrees of freedom; we can walk around on the flat surface of a floor, but we can also climb a hill or jump up in the air. Many times, however, we are restricted to one or two degrees of freedom; for example, when we are driving in a lane along a road, we have one degree of freedom (and sometimes no degrees of freedom if we are hemmed in by traffic and not moving).

The concept of degrees of freedom can also be applied to our lives. We have a certain perception of our lives, how they work and fit together, and often we feel restricted by our circumstances. For example, many of us experience finances as something that limits our freedom of movement, and we feel restricted by our bank balance or by the monetary cost of certain things. Many of us also feel trapped by the need to earn a living, and so a lot of our time is spent doing things we don't really want to be doing. As we age, we may feel physically restricted by our bodies that don't have the same freedom of movement or strength to carry us around that they had when we were younger. Or, at an emotional level, we can feel confined by people's expectations of us or the role that society expects us to play. (I was recently watching a child having a good, loud cry in public, and I longed for the same freedom to stand in the middle of a crowd and just howl my head off. But as an adult, socialization limits my freedom of expression.)

Some of the time, these restrictions are helpful; they are part of learning to lead a responsible adult life that "works" in some way. But these constrictions also tend to pile up and make us feel emotionally paralyzed. Heavy work pressure, family expectations, or even *perceptions* of expectations that we project onto others can all hedge us in. We may also project onto God all sorts of expectations we have learned from the religion with which we grew up.

All these things limit our degrees of freedom. I am especially sad when I consider how much Christianity has been used to restrict people's sense of their freedom of movement. In reality, it should be just the opposite. Paul wrote "It is for freedom that you have been set free, so don't let yourselves be yoked again to slavery" (Galatians 5:1), and Jesus said, "I have come that you may have life to the full" (John 10:10). Jesus also said, "The truth will set you free" (John 8:32).

But what does this mean? What is this truth that will set us free?

I was taught to believe Jesus was talking about doctrinal truth—and yet it seemed to me, as I was growing up, that strict doctrine kept people confined by the need to be right rather than leading them anywhere near actual freedom. Freedom should not be an entry in some imaginary Divine ledger book where we get a checkmark next to the criterion of "freedom." No, it should actually make us *feel* free, like we can take deep breaths of fresh air. Doctrine, however, is much more about being right than it is about being free. To grow spiritually, we have to want to be free more than we want to be right.

I believe the freedom Paul and Jesus spoke of in the verses I just quoted, as well as what all good spiritual teaching guides us toward, is a new degree of freedom, an added depth dimension, that brings a greater sense of spaciousness and ease of movement into our lives. This does not necessarily mean we have enhanced freedom of movement physically; the truth being referred to in these verses is an inner truth, a recognition of what goes on inside us that keeps us stuck.

Recognizing and releasing these stuck areas leads to the spiritual and emotional freedom that allowed Paul to say: "I have learned the secret of being content, whether in plenty or in need" (Philippians 4:11). In other words, this inner freedom cannot be hemmed in by our bank balance or our life circumstances. It is a freedom that releases us from the emotional restrictions we feel from social expectations or materialism or others' opinions, by giving us an inner source of identity rooted in God.

This brings a whole new degree of freedom, an inner freedom of movement that releases us from the constriction of our usual automatic mode—our knee-jerk cravings, defenses, and self-centered reactions. These are what Paul would have described as the "old nature" or "the flesh."

> Those who live according to the flesh have their minds set on what the flesh desires; but those who live in accordance with the Spirit have their minds set on what the Spirit desires. The mind governed by the flesh is death, but the mind governed by the Spirit is life and peace. (Romans 8:5, 6)

The perspective the Spirit brings offers us a much more expansive view of our lives, one that yields a spaciousness that's free from the old restrictions we've placed on ourselves. Those old mental habits no longer need to restrict our inner sense of abundance, well-being, and freedom.

Developing Inner Freedom

A key way to grow our awareness of this expansive view is through times of quiet, open, and receptive listening for the vast and mysterious ways of God. In doing this, we become present to the singular moment that holds us *now,* while at the same time, we let go of the narrative we usually play in our minds. As we recognize and release the virtual reality our minds have spun, we start to make room for the boundless, utterly unconditional loving presence of God.

Imagine being in the sea with wild waves breaking over you. If you stay on the waves' surface level, you may quickly become overwhelmed—but if you dive deeper, beneath the turbulent water, you'll find that everything is peaceful and quiet, and the waves lose their threat. This process of diving deeper is like our journey into God: beneath the surface of life, we discover the vast freedom of God, where we are held, loved, and kept ultimately secure. Through this, we find the freedom of deep contentment and well-being, no matter what the surface restrictions of our lives are.

This movement has been described as falling through our lives' *circumstances* into our real lives. Our actual lives—who we are in God—are expansive, liberated, filled with joy, hope, and love.

To discover the depth dimension, all we have to do is dive down beneath the surface.

Why do you stay in prison
when the door is so wide open?
Move outside the tangle of fear-thinking. Live in silence.
Flow down and down
in always widening rings of being.

—RUMI[2]

INVITATION TO REFLECT

Spend a while sitting still as you focus gently on your breathing, allowing yourself to become quiet inside. Now ask yourself:

- Have you had any experiences of the depth dimension in your life? If so, what did these moments feel like? What were the conditions that led to them? You might find it helpful to reflect on these moments by writing about them in your journal.

- Do you long for greater freedom in your life? What are the circumstances that constrained you? What is the deeper yearning of your heart? Express your heart's cry to God in whatever way you want (for example, through verbal prayer, art, poetry, dance, or music).

Now allow yourself to become quiet again, remaining still, open, and receptive to God for a few more minutes.

NOTES

1. Interview with James Finley, "Awakening Moments," *Radical Discipleship* (June 25, 2017), https://radicaldiscipleship.net.

2. Jelaluddin Rumi. *The Essential Rumi,* Coleman Barks, trans. (San Francisco, CA: HarperCollins, 1995), p. 3.

2

Discovering God in Our Depths

As we move toward our center,
our own being and the divine being
become more and more mysteriously interwoven.

−CYNTHIA BOURGEAULT[1]

When God met Moses in the form of the burning bush, Moses asked for God's name. God's reply was: "I am that I am" (Exodus 3:14). This fascinating name implies that the Divine is the ultimate Present One, the Living One in the here and now.

In the story of Jacob's dream of angels going up and down a stairway into the heavens, we get another hint about the nature of God. "When Jacob awoke from his sleep," the Bible tells us, "he thought, 'Surely the Life-Giver[2] is in this place, and I was not aware of it.'" Jacob went on to say, "How awesome is this place!

This is none other than the house of God; this is the gate of heaven" (Genesis 28:12–17).

Jacob's words can express our own experience: *Surely the Life-Giver is in this place, and I was not aware of it.* God is here and now, the always present I-Am-That-I-Am, but so much of the time we are like Jacob, unaware, asleep to the living Presence of God.

The religious orientation in which many of us grew up focused on our *ideas* about God and about right and wrong. When we try to be religious, we reflect on these ideas—but we miss the *experience* of knowing God. Our religion is theological and moral, rather than experiential. Meanwhile, God is in *this* place, in *this* time; this very moment is the gate of heaven, but we are unconscious.

Not only is God present in this place, this moment, but God is also present within each of us, more intimately woven into our beings than we can imagine. The great German mystic Meister Eckhart wrote, "I am as sure as I live that nothing is so near to me as God. God is nearer to me than I am to myself; my existence depends on the nearness and presence of God."[3] God breathes with our breath and flows through our veins, whether we are aware of it or not.

Etty Hillesum, a Jewish mystic, used a lovely image to describe this: "There is really a deep well inside me. And in it dwells God. Sometimes I am there too. But more often stones and grit block the well, and God is buried beneath. Then He must be dug out again."[4]

The invitation to a deeper journey is the invitation to come to know God directly, not as an intellectual concept but through direct experience. We do this by moving more and more deeply into this interior domain, into this well where God dwells deep within us. Cynthia Bourgeault described the spiritual journey as "awakening in a whole new way to the imperishable scent of your own aliveness. To know yourself deeply and truly, from deep within yourself, is to know God as well."[5]

This is not some New-Age idea that diminishes our sense of God to our own egocentricity. God is not limited by the boundaries of our personalities. As Richard Rohr wrote, "God is both intimate and ultimate." He went on to say:

> When you move to non-dual thinking, God is no longer "out there" but not just "in here" either. . . . In the mystics, God is always experienced in the soul and at the same time as totally beyond and mysterious.[6]

Many of us feel separated from God because we have been looking for God only beyond ourselves, as a separate Being. We've been looking "out there," when all the while, here God is, hidden in the depths of our own beings.

> God is Spirit. That Spirit is the source of life, freedom, harmony, power, and well-being. That Spirit and Source is within you. It's not located **outside** of you somewhere out there; it is inside you. Yes, INSIDE you. Yes, inside YOU.[7]

My Own Inner Journey

In my teens and early adulthood, I was very concerned with "right belief": I wanted to make sure I had the correct doctrine about God. During the years I attended a liberal university, I was challenged to let go of some of this certainty about beliefs, and I started exploring the dimension of intimate relationship with God—being real with God. I gradually learned to be my true self in this relationship, and with that came the wondrous discovery of God's grace that embraces the whole of me unconditionally. As my spiritual experience moved from my head to my heart, I opened myself up to the love of God.

However, I was still trying to find God "out there" somewhere, as a relational presence outside myself. This was a valid and necessary part of my journey, but after a while, I was more and more drawn to finding God in the mysterious spaces that silence and stillness open up. In the process, I lost a sense of "God out there," and this made me sad. Sometimes, I would wake up in the night crying, "Where are you, God?" I remained faithful to my practice of silent prayer, though, trusting it would take me where I needed to go.

Fortunately, during this process, I was involved in the Dove Fellowship, a community of people who together explore this journey into silence. I was also reading the writings of the mystics, who assured me that this loss of a tangible and familiar sense of God is a necessary part of the spiritual journey. I began to experience a sense of God as a holding, grounding reality.

I have had glimmers of God woven into my life so intimately and faithfully that I realize this faithful Presence has been there all along; I just wasn't attuned to it. My inner journey has been a painful, wonderful adventure of discovering this God who is not only out there but also in here, this God who is not separate from me and lording it over the people of this world but a God who is closer to me than I am to myself.

Coming Home to Myself

The inner journey involves being present in our lives, in our bodies, in the present moment. Spirituality is not some outer goal we strive toward but rather a coming-home to ourselves: learning to become present in our lives and going deeper into who and where we are. As we do this, we discover an incredibly rich source of life and nourishment—the place where God resides within each of us. John O'Donohue described this as a:

> place in you where you have *never* been wounded, where there is still a sureness in you, where there's a seamlessness in you, and where there is a confidence and tranquility in you. And I think the intention of prayer and spirituality and love is, now and again, to visit that inner kind of sanctuary.[8]

We can relax into this Presence at the center of our being, rather than groping around for God "out there." On one of my silent retreats, I wrote in my journal:

> THIS moment is the depth dimension into God. By sinking deeper into now, by staying present and open to what IS (whatever arises, even despair or fear), this is how the taproot of my heart sinks into the Fertile Ground of Being. Only this. This is how the well is unblocked. The grit and stones are all the mental grasping and conjecturing that I get trapped in—the church of the poison mind where I worship so often. The simple gesture of noticing and letting go, resigning and returning. This is IT! How slowly, quietly, and surely these trees sink their roots down deep, and life and growth becomes.

The deeper we sink our roots into the Source of Life, and the more we clear away the grit and stones of our own head-noise and self-constructed identity, the more we can become channels for this life to flow through us.

> *Life is a journey to find ourselves,*
> *our God and our own wisdom.*
> *The beginning and end of our journey*
> *is the cave of the heart . . .*
> *the deepest psychological ground of one's being.*

It is the inner sanctuary where self-awareness
goes beyond analytical reflection
and opens out into . . . the Abyss of the unknown
yet always present.
This is the one who is more intimate to us
than we are to ourselves.

—BILL WHITTIER[9]

INVITATION TO REFLECT

Spend a while sitting still and focusing gently on your breathing, allowing yourself to become quiet inside. Then consider these questions. You might find it helpful to write about your responses in your journal.

- What reaction do you have to the idea of God's presence being within you? Does this disturb you in any way? Is this just an idea for you—or do you know it experientially?

- Etty Hillesum described the well within us where God dwells, which is often blocked by grit and stones. Are you aware of any blockages in your own life that prevent you from experiencing the quiet depth of the Presence of God in the well of your own being?

- Is there any sense of deeper longing that has been evoked by the invitation to know God in your depths? Express your response to God in your journal or in whatever way works best for you (verbal prayer, art, poetry, dance, or music).

Now allow yourself to become quiet again, remaining still, open, and receptive to God for a few minutes.

NOTES

1. Cynthia Bourgeault. *Centering Prayer and Inner Awakening* (Cambridge, MA: Cowley, 2004), p. 13.

2. The word traditionally translated in the Hebrew scriptures as "Lord" is actually Yahweh, which according to Hebrew Bible scholars, is a mysterious word with these possible meanings: Life-Giver, the One Who Is Ever Coming into Manifestation, the Self-Existent and Eternal One, Promise Keeper, and Creator.

3. Meister Eckhart. *Meister Eckhart: A Modern Translation*, Raymond Bernard Blankney, trans. (New York: Harper Torchbook, 1941), p. 29.

4. Etty Hillesum. *An Interrupted Life: The Diaries, 1941–1943 and Letters from Westerbork* (New York: Holt, 1996), p. 44.

5. Cynthia Bourgeault. From a talk given at the Living School of Action and Contemplation.

6. Richard Rohr. "God Is Not 'Out There,'" from his Daily Meditations (September 5, 2014), https://cac.org/daily-meditations/.

7. Jim Palmer. *Inner Anarchy: Dethroning God and Jesus to Save Ourselves and the World* (Scotts Valley, CA: CreateSpace Independent Publishing Platform, 2014), (no page available).

8. John O'Donohue. In the interview "The Inner Landscape of Beauty," *On Being with Krista Tippett* (February 28, 2008), https://onbeing.org/.

9. Bill Whittier. *The Journey of a Priest: To Find Himself, His God and His Own Wisdom* (Scotts Valley, CA: CreateSpace Independent Publishing Platform, 2013), (no page available).

3

Faith and Unknowing

We walk by faith, not by sight.

−2 Corinthians 5:7

At some point on our deepening journey, we will have to face some difficult but important questions: *What is faith? What does it mean to walk by faith, not by sight? And how do we know we are on the right path?*

In discussing these questions, let's start with looking at our usual ways of knowing. In our Western world, we have allowed our rational minds to become dominant, and we rely on them to form our ideas about what faith is. Many of us grew up with the assumption that faith means believing the "right things" about God. Any questioning of these beliefs was seen as a loss of faith.

But the rational part of our minds is only one small part of our ability to know, and because we have allowed that part to dominate, we have ended up with an insipid and misguided understanding of faith. We assume our faith should be intellectually defendable and have logical answers to all the questions. But what is the point of faith if it all makes sense to your rational mind and gives you all the answers? This is not faith at all.

In a contemplative group I belong to, one person described some of her own faith questioning this way: "I have been wondering if I have been too naïve in believing what people tell me to believe."

Rather than shoving our heads in the sand and ignoring questions like these, we need to let them rattle our minds. If we are going to experience the faith journey with integrity, it will move us from our entrenched and broad collective ideas into a much more personal, real space—a space where we no longer only believe what people have told us we should believe, but where we find God in a place that's deeper than the old answers can reach. This is why, at some points in our spiritual journeys, we may feel as though we are falling into an abyss. This can be very frightening, because this space is so much deeper and more mysterious than our previous belief systems can adequately explain.

When something shakes the intellectual constructs of our faith, we see where we have been holding on to something that may have worked for a while but has now become a limited image of God. When we place our trust in these mental constructs, we are not necessarily trusting God; instead, we are trusting our *ideas* about God. The journey of deepening trust in God peels away these ideas we held so dearly and closely. This can feel painful, but as we become vulnerable to God in new ways, we move into a deeper, more confident level of trust

The concepts that fall away are like old layers of skin that once served a purpose but we have now outgrown; we are like snakes that need to shed their outer epidermis in order to grow. During these times, we may feel very fragile, but this is precisely what trust requires—not being able to rely on our own coping methods or on the old thought structures to carry us but instead, having to cling to God when everything else feels shaky and frightening. These times of vulnerability are "thin" times, when the layers we usually rely on for protection are gone. This is a deeply transformative space.

This journey of faith away from old certainties and traditional ways of understanding can sometimes feel as if we are following an individualistic tangent, wandering off on our own into odd or dangerous places. It can also be a very lonely process, because of the dismantling of the assumptions that previously gave us a sense of belonging to a community of other people who thought the same way we did. As we leave behind the well-trodden path, we sometimes worry about where we are heading.

Living with Our Questions

Basil Pennington, a Cistercian monk, wrote a wonderful book called *Living in the Question*, in which he discussed our tendency to grab for answers because of our intense discomfort with anything that is unanswered.

> A pat answer is closed, it is finished; that's it. It goes no-where and leaves little room for hope. A question, the mystery, opens the space for us. It is full of possibility. It gives hope of life and ever more abundant life. Our faith, solid as it might be, is full of questions. And therefore full of life and hope.[1]

Learning to live with open questions as we venture down lonely paths is an important part of our deepening faith journeys. In this state of uncertainty, we become acutely aware that we can no longer trust our minds, our religious structures, or our old belief systems; instead, we have to throw ourselves onto God, entrusting ourselves to the Life-Giver. This is where faith really grows. Having a group to support us in this journey, people who don't condemn us or try to change us, can help us hold this space open for our questions and doubts.

I am not saying, though, that this deeper spirituality requires that we completely abandon the constructs of traditional religion. Sometimes, we eventually circle back to some of the core teachings, where we rediscover their essence in much greater depth. These aspects of religious teachings can then become truly life-giving and transformative, rather than being structures we only hold on to in order to conform.

Fruits of the Faith Journey

As we face our own vulnerability and uncertainty, we are less likely to coerce other people to believe things our way or to judge others' behaviors. Instead, as we wend our way ever more deeply into the depth dimension, we begin to experience a generous spaciousness and inner authority. This is true transformation—and we can recognize it by its fruits.

Galatians 5:22 describes these fruits as "love, joy, peace, patience, kindness, generosity, faithfulness, gentleness and self-control." These speak with so much more clarity than the thumping words many people shout in the name of Jesus. These spiritual "fruits" have little do with outward shows of good deeds, with church attendance, or with strict religious observances. They result from real inner transformation, which is the work of God in us, guiding us on this scary, foggy voyage.

Learning to See in the Dark

This brings us to the question of how we come to experientially know the sense of union with God at a deeper level than the rational mind. This is not an intellectual level of knowing; it is very subtle—a knowing that gets imprinted into our being. It is more like an "unknowing knowing."

Anthony de Mello described this unknowing knowing, saying:

Many mystics tell us that, in addition to the mind and heart with which we ordinarily communicate with God, we are, all of us, endowed with a mystical mind and heart, a faculty which makes it possible for us to know God directly, to grasp and intuit him [sic] in his very being, though in a dark manner, apart from all thoughts, concepts and images. . . . When our heart gets its first direct, dark glimpse of God it feels like a glimpse into emptiness and blankness. . . . It requires a good deal of faith to gaze with love and yearning at what seems just like nothing when we first get in touch with it.[2]

This knowing takes place at a deeper level than words can adequately describe, although spiritual teachers have used various phrases and metaphors to try to describe it: "cloud of unknowing,"[3] "a blind stirring of love in our heart,"[4] "a sunlit absence,"[5] or "a breath without breath, an expanseless expanse."[6] Cynthia Bourgeault described this paradoxical awareness as being similar to learning to see in the dark:

At first everything seems totally black. But if you're patient and don't grab for the flashlight, little by little you begin to discover that you can pick out shadows and shapes, and in some mysterious way "see."[7]

The deepening journey therefore requires patience and ongoing practice, so that we can become attuned to the subtle, still, small voice that speaks in the darkness of unknowing knowing. In the second part of this book, we will explore various practices that can be helpful in this journey toward the light.

> *Sometimes [the journey]*
> *means winding through a dark wood.*
> *It doesn't mean we're lost, however.*
> *The darkness is part of the trip.*
> *Too many of us panic in the dark.*
> *We don't understand that it's a holy dark*
> *and that the idea is to surrender to it*
> *and journey through to real light.*
>
> —SUE MONK KIDD[8]

INVITATION TO REFLECT:

Spend a while sitting still and focusing gently on your breathing, allowing yourself to become quiet inside. Then ask yourself:

- Have you been struggling with a loss of certainty or clarity in your faith journey? What are some of the unanswered questions or contradictions you are grappling with? You might find it helpful to write these in your journal.

- Do any of the following descriptions of a deeper knowing resonate with you? Allow yourself to respond to this image in whatever way is most expressive for you (for example, through verbal prayer, art, poetry, dance, or music).

  » cloud of unknowing
  » a blind stirring of love in your heart
  » a sunlit absence
  » a journey through a dark forest
  » learning to see in the dark

Now allow yourself to become quiet again, remaining still, open, and receptive to God for a few minutes.

NOTES

1. M. Basil Pennington. *Living in the Question: Meditations in the Style of Lectio Divina* (New York: Continuum, 1999), p. 2.

2. Anthony de Mello. *Writings* (Maryknoll, NY: Orbis, 1999), p. 30.

3. *The Cloud of Unknowing* is a fourteenth-century book on Christian mysticism that was written anonymously.

4. James Finley often uses this phrase.

5. Author Martin Laird took this phrase from a poem by Seamus Heaney and used it to describe "an expansion within awareness" that happens during contemplation.

6. Meister Eckhart, the thirteenth-century German mystic, used these phrases.

7. Cynthia Bourgeault. *Centering Prayer and Inner Awakening* (Cambridge, MA: Cowley, 2004), p. 16.

8. Sue Monk Kidd. *When the Heart Waits: Spiritual Direction for Life's Sacred Questions* (San Francisco, CA: Harper and Row, 1990), p. 152.

PART II

Inner Transformation

4

Waking Up

We are one blink of an eye away
from being fully awake.

—PEMA CHÖDRÖN[1]

Most of us have had a dream so vivid that for a few moments when we wake up, we can't remember where we are and what is actually happening in our life. If the dream was a nightmare, we'll feel a huge relief to discover it isn't real. While we were in the dream, though, it felt utterly convincing, with the power to evoke terror or even suffering, despite being merely a mental creation.

We can use this as an analogy to help us understand how our minds keep us locked in a fantasy world, a world that isn't actually real. We are constantly building a story around stimuli and events, and then we believe in this version of life our minds have spun. We have to learn that our minds *cannot be trusted to give us an accurate picture of reality*.

Neurobiology research has found that our minds cling to the negative. Tragic or traumatic experiences make a deeper imprint on our brains, shaping our neural network—as well as our impression of reality. The research indicates that no matter how privileged or comfortable our lives are, we will still tend to create a negative narrative in our minds. By contrast, our brains don't hold on to positive experiences as firmly; instead, happy events often slip from our memories.[2] Our negative memories may also be far more detailed than our positive memories. Psychologists think this has evolutionary roots, since, according to Stanford University professor Laura Carstensen, "It's more important for people, for survival, to notice the lion in the brush than it is to notice the beautiful flower that's growing on the other side of the way."[3] As a result of our brains' responses, we often live in a shadowy, nightmare version of life, one we perceive as threatening and withholding.

Our sense of ourselves is often as inaccurate as our perceptions of the world around us. Imagine someone who plays the same character in a theatrical production so long she forgets who she is apart from the character. The word *persona* comes from the Greek *personare,* which was used in Greek theatre to describe the masks actors wore to symbolize the characters they were playing. Carl Jung described the persona as "a kind of mask, designed on the one hand to make an impression on others, and on the other, to conceal the true nature of the individual."[4] In order to develop a fuller picture of our true identities, we need to take off the mask, step back from the play—or wake up from the nightmare—and rediscover who we are without the story.

Habituation and Neuroplasticity

Waking up from the nightmare can be tricky, though. We have lived in our minds' versions of reality and believed in them for so long that they have become hardwired into our brain structure. As neurobiologist Donald Hebb said, "Neurons that fire together wire together."[5] As a result, many of the "choices" we make are not free choices but are instead conditioned responses that have become engineered into our neural structure. The Enneagram and self-awareness practices are tools that can help us see this. When we recognize our patterns of behavior, we can start the process of stepping back and recognizing the roles we have been playing throughout our lives.

In recent months, while doing a great deal of this inner scrutiny, I have sometimes wondered if I have lived my whole life in an echo chamber, replaying destructive patterns over and over without fully recognizing what I was doing. When I identify myself with my patterns, I cannot see them any better than I can see the back of my own neck—but when I step back, becoming a witness to these patterns, then I can see them clearly. Unfortunately, a one-off stepping back doesn't do the trick. The virtual reality my mind has spun—with its many sticky layers, all neurologically enforced—clings to my self-identity.

The waking-up process requires a rewiring of our brains: a disciplined rehabituation of our ways of seeing. Fortunately, neurobiologists have discovered a phenomenon they call *neuroplasticity*, which means the shape of our brains can change if we learn new mental habits.

There's another tricky thing about the waking-up process: the version of our lives that we believe ensnares our entire thinking system. This means we need to find deeper ways of knowing than merely operating at the intellectual level. Our minds have a limited, dualistic way of understanding reality, and for each of us, our frame of reference is ourself. Staying stuck in the mind-level of knowing limits our capacity to see a bigger picture.

Because our logical minds' basic understanding is dualistic—differentiating one object from another, good from bad, me from you—we are trapped in a small picture of who we are. We have limited capacity to know we are already in union with God.

The Good News of the Gospel

This bigger picture of who we are in God is the good news of the gospel, as the following passages illustrate:

> That all of them may be one, Father, just as you are in me and I am in you. May they also be in us. (John 17:21)

> My old self has been crucified with Christ. It is no longer I who live, but Christ who lives in me. (Galatians 2:20)

To them God has chosen to make known among the
Gentiles the glorious riches of this mystery, which is
Christ in you, the hope of glory. (Colossians 1:27)

The old self that has been "crucified with Christ" is the small,
constricted, self-constructed self, which is sometimes also referred
to as the *ego self* or the *false self*. This sense of self has to be gradually
discarded for us to be able to awaken to the spacious, generative Self
that is described as "Christ who lives in me." This is the Self that is
already in union with God—and has never been separate.

Unfortunately, we have been trying to understand the gospel
using the dualistic, egoic operating system, so we have divided it
all up again into us/them, good/bad, saved/unsaved. As Jesus said,
"Though seeing, they do not see; though hearing, they do not hear or
understand" (Matthew 13:13). We are habitually seeing and hearing
in a narrow, mind-dominated, self-referential way. Even our belief
systems are so tangled up in this operating system that we will never
see from a much bigger, fuller perspective until we wake up from the
nightmare. This is the meaning of the Greek word for repentance,
metanoia, which literally means "larger knowing"—knowing from
within a much bigger frame than our usual thought-based way of
knowing.

The real difficulty is that we cannot think our way out of this
operating system. Believe me, I have tried—but it is a closed system,
one that circles back endlessly on itself. We have to recognize what
is happening when we are trapped in our habitual thought patterns

and develop practices that gradually free us from the sticky grip of these cycles.[6]

The Calculating Mind and the Contemplative Mind

In his book *The Naked Now*, Richard Rohr refers to the dualistic egoic way of knowing as the *calculating mind*, and he describes the more spacious, unitive way of knowing as the "contemplative mind."[7] The following table, based on his descriptions of these two ways of knowing, gives an idea of the shift that takes place in this *metanoia* process.

CALCULATING MIND	CONTEMPLATIVE MIND
Outer	**Inner**
• The typical perspective that's brought to day-to-day thinking and processing of life • Concerned with what is happening "out there," caught up in appearances—the surface, concrete level of life (i.e., status, wealth, security, insurance, etc.)	• Knows there is an inner dimension that is much deeper and richer than the surface • Knows that well-being has much more to do with an inner state than with outward forms

CALCULATING MIND	CONTEMPLATIVE MIND
Control	**Has an attitude of surrender / yielding**
• Tries to understand, order, and control life • Incessant need to be right	• Characterized by the ability to let go of control and "go with the flow," be wrong, or even be wronged • Allows for the movement of the Spirit (who always brings greater wisdom, freshness, and expansiveness) • Models Jesus' attitude of "not my will but yours"
Identifies with thoughts	**Recognizes thinking mind but holds it lightly**
• Unaware of being stuck in our thoughts • Sense of identity and what the world is like derived only from thoughts	• Can recognize when thinking is happening • Can let go of obsessive thought patterns
Has an attitude of "change the world to suit my needs"	**Believes "the only person I can change is myself"**
• Blames unhappiness on what other people are doing • Tries to change others to fit in with personal beliefs and opinions	• Recognizes that unhappiness is not the fault of others • Free to respond to situations rather than reacting • Allows for challenges and changes as a result of circumstances rather than trying to fix the situation or others

CALCULATING MIND	CONTEMPLATIVE MIND
Prayer = control	**Prayer = surrender**
• Prayer is used to change God's mind and take control of events.	• Prayer is a practice of surrender, of opening the heart and allowing God access to bring about change.
Awareness of time: past / future / elsewhere	**Awareness of time: the present moment**
• Continually caught up in regrets about the past, anxieties about the future, or what is happening elsewhere	• Knows the only place and time that is real is here and now • Continually returns to the present and is therefore open to the presence of the I-Am, the ever-present One
Focuses on rational knowing	**Includes body and spirit knowing**
• Way of knowing is mind-dominated. • Values linear, logical thinking and order • Leads to transactional thinking: conditional (I'll love you if . . .), exclusionary, giving only to receive	• Way of knowing is intuitive and creative, but "trans-rational." • Lets go of the rational and moves deeper in order to be able to return to the rational with a fresh, inclusive perspective

CALCULATING MIND	CONTEMPLATIVE MIND
Need for certainty and formulaic structures	**Open to paradox and uncertainty, mystery and unknowing**
• Has to "know" for certain (about life and God) • Expects life to follow formulas (e.g., reward / punishment system) • Demands fairness • Mistakes certainty for faith	• Balances knowing with unknowing • Knows that any doctrine / image of God is only a vague sense of God and can never be self-consistent or perfectly true. • Has learned that growth happens through light and darkness, joy and pain • Lets go of the need for fairness, recognizes the deeper economy of unmerited grace (As Richard Rohr says, grace shatters our moral calculus. There is nothing more offensive to the calculating mind than grace, but it characterizes the contemplative mind.)
Dualistic "either / or"	**Non-dual "both / and"**
• Continually assesses for good / bad, right / wrong, desirable / undesirable, insider / outsider • Reinforces a divided, small view of the world and God	• Can hold the bigger field open where everything and everyone belongs • Follows Christ's command to love enemies

CALCULATING MIND	CONTEMPLATIVE MIND
"Small self" identity	**Larger sense of identity in God**
• Entrenched identity as "me" separate from "you," "them," and God	• Knows everything is interconnected • Lets go of boundary lines of self-definition • Experiences abiding union with God and others
Fearful and defensive attitude toward life	**Stable, spacious, and grounded perspective**
• Small identity that's insecure and easily offended, leading to the need to prop up and defend the self • Strong need to protect the small self from humiliation, failure, suffering, and shame • Fearful about the future	• Knows a larger, more spacious and robust identity is held safe in God • Does not have anything to defend because no matter what, the self is held in God • More peaceful and contented, less fearful about the future, because regardless of circumstances, nothing can destroy the identity that is held in God

CALCULATING MIND	CONTEMPLATIVE MIND
Complaining and critical mindset	**Gratitude forms the mental background**
• The fearful and defensive nature of the calculating mind can make it critical and negative. • Typical daily dialogue involves complaining, railing against the events of the day, and criticizing others and self.	• Because the contemplative mind is less threatened and self-involved, it is more positively oriented. • Can recognize the beauty of the moment • Expresses gratitude (This is both a fruit of the contemplative mind and a conscious practice that develops it.)
Resistant to real life	**Receives reality as it is**
• Conditional mode of happiness: "I will be happy if . . ." • Tends to take a resistant stance to life	• Lets go of conditions for happiness, and receives the moment as it is • Allows life to touch, even shake, identity, and thereby move the sense of self deeper into God

CALCULATING MIND	CONTEMPLATIVE MIND
Negative-oriented and problem-solving approach to life	**Appreciative approach to life**
• Sees the problem in most situations • Tries to solve the problems of life (even when this is impossible) • Tries to work out who is to blame • Rails against "bad" situations and people • Internal stance = fight / flight	• Says "yes" to the situation, allowing it to be as it is without judgment • Has the attitude of: "The potentially good thing about this situation is . . ." • Focuses on the perspective of the serenity prayer: "God grant me the serenity to accept the things I cannot change, the courage to change the things I can, and the wisdom to know the difference."
Avoidant or exacerbating of distress	**Remains present in distress**
• Response to distress = avoid, distract, numb, resist • Ongoing narrative with self as the victim / martyr / misunderstood party	• Response to distress = stay with this • Remains present to circumstances as teachers / transformative possibilities: "This is not to be distrusted or avoided but has been sent for my healing."(In Richard Rohr's words, "The contemplative mind lets the terrifying/wonderful moment be what it is."[8]) • Chooses to "feel it" rather than "fuel it"

These descriptors of the contemplative mind are both qualities and practices. The change from the calculating mind to the contemplative doesn't happen overnight through a magical wave of the wand, through a once-off choice, or by applying a set formula. Rather, it is a stance that is gradually lived into through practice; it becomes a pattern within our being.

For example, choosing to remain present to our emotions in times of distress allows us to learn experientially that the distressing emotions aren't as threatening as we originally thought they would be. This in turn allows us to further develop the ability to remain present in distress. Similarly, making the choice to love our enemies, rather than judging or criticizing them, loosens the boundaries we have erected against our enemies—and this allows our hearts to open in compassion, which in turn allows us to love our enemies with genuine affection.

Personal Reflections on the Contemplative Mind

I have often noticed the cramped grip of my calculating mind and how powerful it can be. When I am in my car and see what other drivers are doing, I catch myself judging people and grousing in my head about poor drivers and lawlessness. When I think about some of the problems in my home nation of South Africa or in the larger world, my mind goes through incessant problem-solving or blaming loops, none of which I am able to do anything about. This obsessive thinking is a useless waste of energy and keeps me stuck in negative, egotistical thinking habits. But as I recognize these patterns and instead choose to soften and open, a gradual transformation takes place. The more I practice this, the more possible it becomes to do it in each moment.

I recently had the privilege of traveling to various southern African rural communities in Zimbabwe, Tanzania, and Mozambique for an evaluation project. This project mostly involved work with out-of-school or unemployed youth from extremely disadvantaged areas, many of whom are orphaned or HIV positive. This was a wonderful opportunity to meet people I would ordinarily never have encountered—but it was also very difficult, as I saw firsthand the depth of suffering, poverty, and hopelessness that many youth face in southern African countries. The people I met and the oppressive sociopolitical contexts in some of the countries weighed heavily on me.

Immediately after one of these trips, I traveled to the United States for the Living School "week-intensive." On one of the mornings, Richard Rohr encouraged us to do a contemplative walk in Nature, dialoguing with some aspect of Nature to see where that would take us. Although it was summer, with green grass and trees, my eyes were drawn to the dry, brown abandoned leaves lying on the grass. The leaves triggered in me an overwhelming sense of despair as I was reminded of the abandoned lives I had just seen, the young people's lost dreams and hopes. The dead leaves also brought to mind the abandoned places in myself I had been recognizing and working with. The dead leaves somehow merged with the sense of hopelessness I felt about changing my stuck ego patterns, as well as the hopelessness I had seen in southern Africa's disenfranchised young people. The leaves that had fallen on parking lots and sidewalks bothered me most with their utter futility; instead of becoming part of the life-cycle of Nature, they would be discarded far away somewhere.

As I carried this sense of utter futility and hopelessness in my heart, I was reminded of a poem titled "The Healing Time" by Pesha Joyce Gertler:

> Finally on my way to yes
> I bump into
> all the places
> where I said no
> to my life
> all the untended wounds
> the red and purple scars . . .
> and I lift them
> one by one
> close to my heart
> and I say holy,
> holy.[9]

And so, as my tear-flooded gaze fell on those dry, abandoned leaves, I spoke over each of them: "Holy, holy." As I did this, I had a sense of also saying this to my memory of each of the young faces I had encountered, to my troubled, beloved country South Africa, and to my own lost, wounded self.

Although no answers came to me, this was a deeply sacred and healing moment. It opened a doorway to a place where I could hold the parts of myself that feel abandoned, out of place, and hopelessly lost. It also felt like an invitation to hold the unanswered questions, broken lives, and painful contradictions of the southern African countries as sacred—not as problems to be solved or people to be blamed but as holy ground to be walked on in humility and to be fully engaged in.

Each of us is invited to open ourselves to the gritty, wonderful reality of life as it is, with all of its pain and contradictions. We don't need to know the why or the how. We can stop blaming the "villains" and trying to solve the world's problems with our small, calculating minds.

The contemplative mind asks us to let go of our resistance or imagined control, and fall again and again into the mystery and spacious beauty of God, the Creator who holds us and everyone in every moment. In that wide-open space, we discover we don't have to understand life or know how everything fits together. This is where we experience true, radical freedom—and the amazing reality that "all shall be well, and all shall be well, and all manner of things shall be well."[10]

As the practice becomes
more and more established in you
so that this inner sanctuary
begins to flow out into your life,
it becomes more and more a place you come from.
It is a bedrock of spiritual intelligence,
a sense of connectedness
known from so deeply within you
that nothing can shake it.

—Cynthia Bourgeault[11]

INVITATION TO REFLECT

Spend a while sitting still and focusing gently on your breathing, allowing yourself to become quiet inside. Then consider the following questions:

- Have you noticed any habitual ways in which your calculating mind reacts to life? (You might find it helpful to look over the table of descriptors of the calculating mind again.) Reflect on some of these in your journal.

- Can you think of ways you might ease the grip of your calculating mind, in some of the typical everyday situations you encounter? How can you allow the more spacious contemplative mind to emerge in these situations? What would your responses look like?

Now allow yourself to become quiet again, remaining still, open, and receptive to God for a few minutes.

NOTES

1. Pema Chödrön. *Start Where You Are: A Guide to Compassionate Living* (Boulder, CO: Shambhala Publications, 2018), p. 1.

2. You can read about this research in Rick Hanson's *Just One Thing: Developing a Buddha Brain One Simple Practice at a Time* (Oakland, CA: New Harbinger, 2011). For a more scholarly overview of the research on negative memories versus positive, see Elizabeth A. Kensinger's "Remembering the Details: Effects of Emotion," *Emotion Review 1*(2: 2009), pp. 99–113.

3. Quoted in Allie Caren, "Why We Often Remember the Bad Better Than the Good," *Washington Post* (November 1, 2018), https://www.washingtonpost.com/science.

4. Carl Jung. *The Collected Works,* vol. 7, Gerhard Adler and R. F.C. Hull, trans. (Princeton, NJ: Princeton University Press, 1972), p. 305.

5. Friedrich Miescher Institute for Biomedical Research. "How Neurons That Wire Together Fire Together," *Neuroscience News,* December 23, 2021, https://neurosciencenews.com.

6. From Part III of this book onward, we will explore a range of practices that help us participate with the *metanoia* movement from our constricted ego sense of self and reality to the more spacious and

generous kind of knowing that is possible when we are freed from our ordinary awareness.

7. Richard Rohr. *The Naked Now: Learning to See as the Mystics See* (Chestnut Ridge, NY: Crossroad, 2009).

8. Richard Rohr. Adapted from the CAC webcast, "What Is the Emerging Church" (November 8, 2008).

9. Pesha Joyce Gertler. *The Healing Time: Finally on My Way to Yes,* chapbook (Columbus, OH: Pudding House Publications, 2008).

10. Julian of Norwich. *Revelations of Divine Love,* available at https://www.catholicspiritualdirection.org/revelations.pdf.

11. Cynthia Bourgeault. *Centering Prayer and Inner Awakening* (Cambridge, MA: Cowley Publications, 2004), p. 17

5

Freedom from Captivity

The Spirit of the Lord is on me,
because he has anointed me to proclaim good news to the poor.
He has sent me to proclaim freedom for the prisoners
and recovery of sight for the blind, to set the oppressed free,
to proclaim the year of the Lord's favor.

–LUKE 4:18-19

Jesus came to proclaim freedom for the prisoners and to set the oppressed free. But this raises the question of what—or who—imprisons us? What oppresses us, and what does real freedom mean?

In Paul's second epistle to the Corinthians, he provides an image that helps us understand our problem:

> For God, who said, "Let light shine out of darkness,"
> made his light shine in our hearts to give us the light of
> the knowledge of God's glory displayed in the face of

Christ. But we have this treasure in jars of clay to show that this all-surpassing power is from God and not from us. (4:6–7)

We have this incredible treasure in our hearts—the light of the knowledge of God—but we don't know it as a lived, ongoing reality. We don't live it, because we are too caught up in the container that holds it. Our prison is the jar of clay, the "me" we each think we are—our ego selves, false selves, or self-serving selves.

The Container of the Self

During the first half of life, we build the container of the self, as Richard Rohr explained in his book *Falling Upward*. We learn to do what is right, we go on our heroic journeys to "make something" of ourselves, we try to be successful at our work and in our families, and some of us work to be good disciples of Jesus. Although this is appropriate during this first portion of our lives, "the container is not an end in itself," as Richard Rohr said, "but exists for the sake of your deeper and fullest life, which you largely do not know about yourself!"[1]

At some point, this container necessarily begins to crack, as we realize life is so much more painful and messy than our formulas or beliefs can explain. This cracking is an opportunity for growth. We are not always correctly guided through this time, though, or we think the jars of clay are all we are, so in desperation, some of us try to clutch at the crumbling containers, using glue and tape to hold them together, painting over the cracks so that everything looks okay. But as Leonard Cohen sings, cracks are necessary to let the light in.[2]

So the gaping contradictions, questions, and messiness of life present us with opportunities to allow ourselves to gradually, bit by bit, let go of the container of the self, so we can wake up to who we really are—the Self we are in union with God, the Self who is filled with the light of the knowledge of God and is able to radiate this light. This is the treasure within the jar of clay.

Unfortunately, this is not as easy or obvious as it sounds. Our sense of identity is wrapped up tightly with the external false self. We think we *are* the clay jars. Meanwhile, we are held captive in the prison of self; if we notice our mind's habits, we quickly recognize that all our thoughts are self-serving, even our thoughts about other people. Ultimately, even our "caring" actions are often done to make people like us, to keep our world in some kind of order, or to convince ourselves and others that we are good, thoughtful people.

We get identity from the strangest places. One of mine is that of being a victim of my past, and this keeps me wrapped up in my story and my wounds. Some people get identity from being right and responsible in a world that's falling apart. Others get identity from being politically correct or being the defenders of the latest cause or victim. All these identities are self-serving; they make us the star of our own show (the one we are constantly narrating in our heads), even if that star is an antihero.

Our thoughts and images of God are also caught up in this self-serving system. I clutch tightly to the security I get from "my God" who takes care of my well-being and the well-being of my family, my ethnic group, my religious denomination (or even my favorite sports team). The ego coopts religion in its quest for defining and defending the self. This is one of the most dangerous pitfalls in our faith journeys, for the ego loves to be right, and so it defends its ideas about religious doctrine. We feel so righteous while doing this, but it is just another clever, self-serving game the ego plays to keep itself in control. Meanwhile, our images of God can be limiting and even destructive. When we cling to them too tightly, they rob us of real encounters with the transcendent God, and they disguise the vulnerability of our nakedness before God. Our fixed ideas about God can keep us from the humility of acknowledging that what we don't know about God is infinitely greater than what we actually do know about God.

Although we often blame our life circumstances for our negative emotional reactions, our circumstances are not really the prisons in which we live. Instead, our *reactions* to circumstances are what imprison us. What truly disturbs us are the stories we tell ourselves and constantly embellish. They lock us into patterns of behavior that limit our spiritual growth, while at the same time, they reinforce our habitual way of reacting to life and our familiar sense of self.

Freeing ourselves from this prison of self is not a conceptual process we can reason our way through, nor can we simply read about it, no matter how profound the reading matter is. Our thoughts—the same part of our minds that reasons and reads—keep us imprisoned. They whirl about, feeding us information that is unhelpful and often faulty (since we have so many blind spots about ourselves and can never see the big picture). We are often convinced we can solve the problem ourselves if only we hit on the right formula or way of understanding the problem.

Speaking from my own experience, I have tried and tried to change some of my patterns of thoughts and behavior, to no avail. If we try to fix our wiring using that same wiring, we just exacerbate the whole problem. And to top it all off, we don't even know the extent to which we are imprisoned in the closed system of the self. We assume that what we see and understand is the truth, and we make the mistake of believing what our thoughts tell us. We believe our version of the story of our life and the world. And so we continually reinforce the very prison we are trapped in.

Resolutions for change or self-improvement don't work in the long run. They might change a few surface issues, but at a deeper level, the self we think we are still remains intact. All we are doing is taping over the gaping cracks in the crumbling jar. Every attempt of ours to fix ourselves is part of the closed prison system we are caught in. As Paul wrote, quoting from the Hebrew scriptures:

There is no one righteous, not even one; there is no one who understands; there is no one who seeks God. All have turned away, they have together become worthless; there is no one who does good, not even one. (Romans 3:10–12).

Isaiah 64:6 states the problem very simply: "our righteousness is as filthy rags."

After trying numerous self-improvement projects, if we are honest with ourselves, we finally realize there is no way we can fix the problem—because we eventually have to admit that the self we think we are *is* the problem! As Paul wrote: "I do not understand what I do. For what I want to do I do not do, but what I hate I do" (Romans 7:15).

Freedom from the Prison of Self

Jesus taught about the need to die to self, to give away our lives: "Whoever tries to keep their life will lose it, and whoever loses their life will preserve it" (Luke 17:33). He demonstrated this truth in his own life and in his death, letting go of everything on the cross. Jesus' embodiment in this world demonstrates that only when we completely let go of the self, as well as all our own attempts to deal with the problems the self creates, can our deepest, truest selves— who we are in God—emerge.

God's solution to the endless mess of self-entrapment is the ultimate Trojan horse: "it is Christ in you, the hope of glory" (Colossians 1:27). This is the treasure in the jar of clay—God dwelling within us, uniting us to God-Self, expressing the light of Christ in and through us. In this Divine indwelling, we discover a more selfless, spacious, and free sense of who we are. To the ego-self, though, this treasure feels like nothing, like death and loss, because it operates at a completely different level from the ego-self's comfort zone. This is why Jesus emphasized giving away our life, using language that referred to the great reversal:

- "So the last will be first, and the first will be last." (Matthew 20:16)

- "Truly I tell you, whatever you did for one of *the least of these* brothers and sisters of mine, you did for me." (Matthew 25:40)

- "Truly I tell you, unless you change and become like little children, you will never enter the kingdom of heaven." (Matthew 18:3)

- "Very truly I tell you, unless a kernel of wheat falls to the ground and dies, it remains only a single seed. But if it dies, it produces many seeds." (John 12:24)

"It is no longer I who live," Paul wrote, "but Christ who lives in me" (Galatians 2:20). The "I" that I think I am, this clay jar of my strategizing, self-serving self, has to be cracked open, bit by bit, to allow the hidden treasure of Christ, who lives in me, to be revealed. Contemplative practices *chip away at our clay jars because they require that we regularly make the choice to let go of our own self-serving agendas and say "yes" to God's presence and action inside us.*

Jens Soering, who is serving a life sentence for a crime he denies having committed, wrote a book about the freedom he found through engaging in contemplative practices while in prison. In the introduction, he wrote:

> The purpose of this book is to remind you of one way to lose your chains. You already know this way, for it is Christ's: he chose to become a prisoner, went willingly to his execution, and thereby overcame the world. If we obey his call, "Follow me," we too may find that the very fetters that now bind us are leading us to a greater freedom. . . . Christ gave us a road map to this path when he said, "If anyone would come after me, he must deny himself and take up his cross and follow me." . . . These [contemplative] techniques liberate us, not by breaking our bonds, but by melting away the self that feels bound. Once the wrists vanish, the manacles fall to the ground and we are free.[3]

This freedom from the prison of self is not a one-time realization that leaves us perfect and holy. Instead, we are invited into a gradual process of learning a whole new habit of being, of knowing who we are without the confines of the outer identity, the self-serving self. As my own contemplative practice has deepened, I have had tastes of this, but I find my ordinary awareness quickly returns—and then there I am, analyzing and trying to understand everything. Before I know it, I am caught up in the strategies of my egoic self again. So I have to keep coming back to this place of unknowing—of letting go of all my strategies, my thoughts, plans, and theories—and return to resting in open receptivity in the presence of God.

Although this is a step-by-step dying process, it is also mysteriously, step-by-step, a life-giving process. The great death-resurrection pattern Jesus showed us is lived out in a spiral kind of way in our own lives, as a gradual unwrapping of the gift of who we are, slowly but surely. The clay jar has to crumble to reveal the treasure within. Each step of dying leads to a deeper sense of freedom and awakening. Macrina Wiederkehr describes this process as "a dying that is full of living, a death that is life-giving,"[4] and the poet Milarepa wrote, "The precious pot containing my riches becomes my teacher in the very moment it breaks."[5]

Each time we let go of our will, surrendering to God's higher way, we weaken the false self's grip on our sense of who we are. We will never completely lose the clay jar: it is part of being human, and the beauty of our unique containers reveal Christ. As we practice letting go, though, we will learn to live more and more lightly with the containers, as we discover in increasing depth and continuity who we are in God. The treasure within each of us will become more and more visible as we allow these clay jars to be the battered, cracked, beautiful, unique human vessels they are.

Love is
The funeral pyre
Where I have laid my living body.
All the false notions of myself
That once caused fear, pain,
Have turned to ash
As I neared God.
What has risen
From the tangled web of thought and sinew
Now shines with jubilation
Through the eyes of angels
And screams from the guts of Infinite existence
Itself.
Love is the funeral pyre
Where the heart must lay
Its body.

—Hafiz[6]

INVITATION TO REFLECT

Spend a while sitting still and focusing gently on your breathing, allowing yourself to become quiet inside. Then think about these questions:

- Are there any circumstances in your life that recently have felt contradictory, painful, or unbearable?

- What is being asked of you? What is being stripped away? How is your identity being challenged through this?

Note any emotions that arise in you as you reflect. You may want to write your answers in your journal. Be gentle with whatever arises, and allow yourself to be held in the tender embrace of God as you face these questions.

Finally, allow yourself to become quiet again, remaining still, open, and receptive to God for a few minutes.

NOTES

1. Richard Rohr. *Falling Upward: A Spirituality for the Two Halves of Life* (Hoboken, NJ: Wiley, 2011), p. 1.

2. Leonard Cohen. "Anthem," from the album *The Future* (Columbia, 1992.)

3. Jens Soering. *The Way of the Prisoner: Breaking the Chains of Self Through Centering Prayer and Centering Practice* (New York: Lantern Books, 2003), p. xxi.

4. Macrina Wiederkehr. *Abide: Keeping Vigil with the Word of God* (Collegeville, MN: Liturgical Press, 2011), ch. 1 (no page available).

5. Quoted in "Breaking Open in the Bardo" by Pema Khandro Rinpoche, *Lion's Roar: Buddhist Wisdom for Our Time* (January 22, 2022), https://www.lionsroar.com/. Milarepa was an eleventh- and twelfth-century Tibetan yogi whose personal life story followed the familiar progression from self-centered confusion to the clarity of self-abandonment.

6. Hafiz. *The Gift: Poems by Hafiz, the Great Sufi Master,* translation by Daniel Ladinsky (New York: Penguin Compass, 1999), p. 69.

6

The Great Unraveling

Unless a grain of wheat falls into the earth and dies,
it remains alone; but if it dies,
it bears much fruit.

—JOHN 12:24

Often on silent retreats, in the lostness and loneliness I invariably experience at some point, I am brought back to the image of the seed stripped of everything until it is a tiny, naked thing, buried in the dark unknowing of the ground. Although the seed is seemingly lost and hidden, it is the place where germination can take place.

Our own undoing—our times of greatest lostness, failure, humiliation, or despair—can be the most important and transformative moments in our inner journey of awakening. The powerful image Christianity gives us is the death-resurrection journey of Jesus, where we see the failure and humiliation of the cross leading to new life and hope. We have tended to theologize this as something Jesus did on our behalf, a transactional act of redemption that allows us to remain passive recipients, rather than as something that challenges us to actively undergo the same process of searing pain, loss, and even devastation.

YES

Our outer layers are difficult to recognize and do not give way easily, but this does not mean we should inflict upon ourselves self-imposed suffering. Instead, God and life are constantly colluding together, in a faithful process of bringing to us exactly what we need to awaken.

Participation with the Unraveling

What is needed from our side during this unraveling process is recognition, participation, and the patience of waiting.

> *Recognition* asks that we look more deeply at whatever happens in our lives, seeing the potential of each situation to contribute to our inner transformation. This is where wise spiritual guidance is needed, and there is too little of it in the typical church-speak that has merged with Western capitalist values of meritocracy (Divine favors for good behavior and prosperity as a sign of God's blessing). We need to help each other

recognize the rich possibilities that lie within every life circumstance, including the painful humiliations and frustrating failures.

Participation means we do not resist what is happening, with that familiar clenching of the gut and blaming of others, but rather we choose to soften and open to whatever the gift may be, in any circumstance. The most painful situations can be the most precious gifts, if we allow them to do their work of undoing, which is vital for new growth to take place.

Sometimes this involves *waiting*, staying with our unresolved dilemmas and unanswered questions, not trying to *work on them*, as much as allowing them to *work on us*, to soften and crack our hard outer shells so that new growth can emerge.

Growth is seldom linear; it takes place in cycles, and sometimes we have to revisit the same place several times before we recognize where we are stuck and need to grow. As Sue Monk Kidd wrote, "By repeatedly entering the spiral of separation, transformation, and emergence, we're brought closer each time to wholeness and the True Self."[1]

Metamorphosis

Another powerful metaphor for inner transformation is the process of metamorphosis: the caterpillar entering the cocoon, waiting in the dark for a while, and emerging as a butterfly. A caterpillar moves by creeping along the ground; it has very little freedom of movement, and its life consists of crawling, eating, and pooping. It's a fairly self-centered and destructive life—at least according to my vegetable garden—that's all about the survival of the caterpillar. But a time comes when the caterpillar has to let go of that way of life and enter the cocoon.

In our own lives, "cocoon periods" require letting go of the old, known way of being (with both ourselves and with God) and submitting to a time of apparent lostness, questioning, and not-knowing. From an external perspective, this may look like humiliation, failure, loss of a career, loss of relationships, loss of respect, and all the other difficult possibilities we resist so strongly. We can rail against these events and become stuck and bitter—or, if we have wise guidance, we can recognize them as opportunities, invitations to let go of the old and enter the cocoon's time of questioning and waiting. This isn't easy, but it holds the promise of a fuller life.

Inside the cocoon, the caterpillar hangs in a dark, cramped little space. Here it dies to its previous form; if you were to cut open the cocoon, all you would find is a formless green goo. The caterpillar completely comes apart, but in this process, it is transformed into something beautiful with wings to fly. The new version is made from *exactly the same cells* as the caterpillar was, but it has been transformed by the process of leaving behind the old and waiting in the dark. As Sue Monk Kidd wrote:

> Bright wings don't just happen. . . . Crisis, change, all the myriad upheavals that blister the spirit and leave us groping—they aren't voices simply of pain but also of creativity. And if we would only listen, we might hear such times beckoning us to a season of waiting, to the place of fertile emptiness. . . . In the stayed-ness of waiting we find everything we need in order to grow. Suspended upside-down in the heart of the question, we touch the sacred spaces of real becoming.[2]

It is all too easy to set up camp in the cocoon. The larger reality that lies beyond it is too vast and unknown, too frightening. *What if my wings don't work properly? What if I have weird colors that my old caterpillar friends won't like? Where will I sleep? What if I miss eating the vegetable garden? What if the world is falling apart out there? It feels so safe and known in here. I think I'll just stay put for now.*

Eventually, the pressure gets to be too much. We either die a slow death inside our cocoons, endlessly self-medicating, watching hours of television, or getting repeatedly sucked into the rabbit hole of social media—or we take the risk to break out of the known, to spread our wings and fly into a new dimension of freedom and wildness.

Feeling uncomfortably squeezed is a wake-up call. As David Whyte wrote, "Anything that doesn't bring you alive is too small for you."[3] The places where we have always looked for our answers and identity are no longer big enough. We need a larger worldview, an expanded sense of who we are and who God is, and a wider perspective on the possibilities and potentials of our lives.

Butterflies no longer live for their own survival: they lay eggs, and they pollinate flowers. In other words, they give life, rather than just munching it for themselves. As we discover new dimensions of freedom, we too build stronger and wider interconnections between ourselves and the entire world around us.

From Coal to Diamond

Let's look at one more example from Nature: that of coal turning to diamond. Coal is dirty, dull, and easily shattered—but when it is buried for a long time and subjected to heat and pressure, it is transformed into a brilliant, unbreakable diamond. Diamond and coal are made of *exactly the same chemical components*, but the rearrangement that happens through heat and pressure, over extremely long time periods, transforms the structure of these chemicals from something weak and grimy into something invincible and bright.

We cannot, however, bring about this kind of change by willing it or trying to control it. Our human tendency is to try to improve ourselves, to will ourselves to be better by being other than we are, a more perfect version of ourselves. Meanwhile, God's grace is the most effective way to transform the stuff we are made of, including our greatest "flaws," turning them into our most precious gifts. This is the difference between true inner transformation and our own attempts at creating outer change through sheer self-discipline and willpower. Inner transformation is a profound and mysterious process we surrender to (as opposed to our attempts to fix our skewedness using the same skewedness, leading to even worse skewedness!).

The Unexpected Gifts of Life

I have become convinced that *every* situation in life has the potential for our growth and transformation, especially the difficult parts—if we choose to soften and welcome rather than resist what is happening. Everything that comes to us is an invitation to let go of our ego-control and self-centered narrowness, and therefore, each circumstance is a possibility for growth into a larger, more robust and free self in God.

The Sufi poet Rumi wrote about a priest who used to pray for muggers and thieves. The priest explained his behavior by saying:

Because they have done me such generous favors. Every
time I turn back toward the things they want, I run into

them. They beat me and leave me in the road, and I understand again, that what they want is not what I want.

Those that make you return, for whatever reason, to the Spirit, be grateful to them. Worry about the others who give you delicious comfort that keeps you from prayer.[4]

The images of the seed coming apart so new life can emerge, the caterpillar waiting in the cocoon, and coal being buried in the ground are invitations to a truly awakened, resurrected life that is robust and beautiful. The dismantling process feels threatening, especially if our identity is strongly rooted in our outer layers—our accomplishments, our work identities, our worthy causes, what we have, and what others think of us—but humiliations and failure contribute to the transformation process.

Humus means "ground," so humiliation means to be returned to the ground—buried, just as the seed or the coal is buried before transformation. This is why God doesn't shield us from failure, humiliation, or other forms of suffering, making our lives smooth or easy, but instead, allows us to reach moments of desperation and despair, so that we are ready to let go of our ego-trappings and our own efforts at getting this life right. Only then will we surrender to the much larger, more mysterious work of transformation. Much of this work happens in a slow, hidden way, and we will need to allow hope to gradually dawn on us as we wait. Sue Monk Kidd wrote:

The fullness of one's soul evolves slowly. We're asked to go within to gestate the newness God is trying to form; we're asked to collaborate with grace. . . waiting provides the time and space necessary for grace to happen. Spirit needs a container to pour itself into. Grace needs an arena in which to incarnate. Waiting can be such a place, if we allow it.[5]

A vital part of inner work, therefore, is to simply become still, to trust the silence and the waiting. Instead of coming to God with the kind of prayers that are actually long monologues outlining our wish lists, we need to attune our inner ears to the more subtle stirrings of God. We weave a sense of expectancy into our lives as we trust the mystery of God's work within us. And all the while, God waits with us and in us, in the core of our beings, in the sacred stillness of our waiting.

> *I will become humble and turn into soil*
> *so your flowers can grow in me. . . .*
> *I came to this earth so that I can find the way back*
> *to my Beloved.*
>
> —RUMI[6]

INVITATION TO REFLECT

Spend a while sitting still and focusing gently on your breathing, allowing yourself to become quiet inside.

Then take some time to consider the three images of inner transformation we explored in this chapter: the seed buried in the ground in order to germinate, the caterpillar in the cocoon where it becomes a butterfly, and coal that transforms into diamond through a long time of heat and pressure. Which of these images resonate most with you? Spend some time allowing your imagination to play with the image.

Then ask yourself: What stage in the process of transformation am I going through at this moment? Write your answer in your journal.

Next, ask yourself: What am I struggling with most at this moment? What is the longing of my heart? Express your heart's cry to God in whatever way is most expressive for you (for example through verbal prayer, art, poetry, dance, or music).

Now allow yourself to become quiet again, remaining still, open, and receptive to God for a few minutes.

NOTES

1. Sue Monk Kidd. *When the Heart Waits: Spiritual Direction for Life's Sacred Moments* (San Francisco, CA: HarperOne, 2016), p. 78.

2. Ibid, p. 12.

3. David Whyte. "Sweet Darkness," *The House of Belonging* (Langley, WA: Many Rivers Press, 1997), p. 23.

4. Quoted in Jack Kornfield, *A Path with Heart: A Guide Through the Perils and Promises of Spiritual Life* (New York: Bantam Books, 1993), p. 74.

5. Kidd, p. 13.

6. Jalāl al-Dīn Rūmī. *Hidden Music*, Azima Melita Kolin and Maryam Mafi, trans. (London, UK: Thorsons, 2001), (no page number available).

7

Enwombed

Jesus replied, "Very truly I tell you,
no one can see the kingdom of God
unless they are born again."
"How can someone be born when they are old?"
Nicodemus asked. "Surely they cannot enter
a second time into their mother's womb to be born!"
Jesus answered, "Very truly I tell you,
no one can enter the kingdom of God
unless they are born of water and the Spirit.
Flesh gives birth to flesh,
but the Spirit gives birth to spirit."

—JOHN 3:3-7

In this passage of scripture, Jesus invites us into a rebirth, a re-creation, responding to God's promise to make all things new. When Jesus referred to being born of the Spirit, he was speaking in Aramaic, and in that language, the word for Spirit is *Ruah*, a feminine word. This absolutely makes sense when we think about birth. How are we born, if not from a mother? Unfortunately, in the many years that patriarchy dominated our theology, many of us have missed out on the essential part the Mother-image plays in this whole process. God is a Mother who births us.

One of the Hebrew words for mercy and compassion is *raham*, which shares a root with the Hebrew word for womb (*rehem*). Since early Hebrew had no vowels, these two words were spelled in exactly the same way. This word is used in various places in scripture to indicate tender compassion or mercy, as in these examples:

> "You will arise and have compassion [*raham*] on Zion, for it is time to show favor to her; the appointed time has come." (Psalm 102:13)

> "Can a mother forget the baby at her breast and have no compassion [*raham*] on the child she has borne?" (Isaiah 49:15)

This word for mercy has sometimes been translated as "enwombedness," implying the bond between a mother and the child in her womb, a nurturing, tender, intimate, and all-consuming love. One of the names for God used in Jewish liturgy is *El Rachum*, which means, literally, "wombed one." In our patriarchal culture, we have overlooked this image of God as our

Birth-Mother, and our understanding of the spiritual journey has suffered as a result.

The Birthing Process

The birth process begins when a zygote, a single fertilized cell, travels down the mother's fallopian tubes. This tiny seed of new life is already growing, and once it reaches the mother's womb, it will be implanted, buried in the nourishing uterine lining. The embryo in the womb is then fed via the umbilical cord, with the mother's blood flowing through the growing fetus, nurturing it and even breathing for it.

When we apply this image to the process of spiritual transformation, we realize our burial is not, after all, in cold, hard ground but rather in the womb of God, where we are held safely and nurtured into fullness of life. God's blood runs through our veins, God's breath breathes in our lungs, and our heartbeats are intimately matched with the rhythm of God's heartbeat. There's nothing we have to do to make this happen—it's already occurring, all on its own—but we need to experience it and allow it to transform our sense of ourselves. We realize we are not separate autonomous beings who are doing it all ourselves; instead, we are held, nurtured, and completely surrounded by God, intimately connected with God's very Being.

The fetus in the womb is utterly dependent on the mother for nurturance and protection. There is no effort it needs to make; it doesn't need to earn its safety or work hard to achieve growth. We too need to recognize our own absolute poverty in our inability to grow ourselves. We have to learn to be quiet, patient, and consenting, giving our "yes" to whatever God is doing in our lives.

Some time ago, I had to do something that felt almost impossibly difficult. One day while I was praying about it, I sensed I was being held in God's womb. I realized then that whatever life brings, it is all part of the process of being fed by the Divine umbilical cord. I was being invited to trust whatever happens as the feeding and nurturance I need for growth (even *this*!). Painful, difficult things will happen in life—but trust knows that everything that happens is an opportunity for growth, "worked together for our good" (Romans 8:28), if we remain open and receptive to the work of God in our lives.

The mother's perspective can also be applied to our spiritual lives. Pregnancy, the time of gestation, is filled with anticipation, as the mother waits for the new life to be born into the world. In our spiritual journeys, we too may have times of hushed expectation, the sense that we are on the brink of something new. *Kairos* is a Greek word that describes these moments; it is time outside of linear time, a sacred moment of readiness for growth or action. We need to be attentive to kairos moments. In times of quiet reflection, as we listen to the deeper stirrings of the Spirit, we ready ourselves for the births that are to come.

Pregnancy is an exciting and joyful time, but for the mother, it can also be a period of discomfort and physical challenge, a time of frustration and impatience. It requires that she submit to and cooperate with the process going on within her. We too may experience similar sensations and emotions as we wait for the new life within us to come to maturity.

Father Bede Griffiths, a Benedictine monk who went to India and started a monastery-ashram, had a mystical experience at the age of eighty after a stroke. He heard a voice say, "Surrender to the Mother." In an interview, he explained:

> God is not simply in the light, in the intelligible world, in the rational order, but God is in the darkness, in the womb, in the Mother, in the chaos from which the order comes. So the chaos is in God, we could say, and that is why discovering darkness is so important. We tend to reject it as evil and as negative and so on, but darkness is the womb of life.[1]

These times of upheaval and inner torment emerge from the creative birth-center of God. The same force that birthed the universe (what scientists speculate was the Big Bang) is at work in our inner beings. Stars, galaxies, planets, and infinite life forms all emerged from the primordial creative Mystery that still underlies and gives birth to everything.

The psalmist expressed this image of being enwombed in God as our Birth Mother:

> For you are creating my inmost being, here and now;
> you are knitting me together in my mother's womb.
> I praise you because I am being fearfully and wonderfully
> made; your works are wonderful, I know that full well.
> (Psalm 139:13, 14, my paraphrase, based on the origi-
> nal Hebrew)

In the midst of ordinary life, with all its joy and pain, order and chaos, through everything that happens, God is knitting us together in our Mother's Womb. This massively creative yet intimate energy is forming our inmost beings, bringing about a newness of life. Nothing is wasted, and everything belongs,[2] if we open our hearts, entrusting ourselves to this becoming, this sacred unfolding.

> *Birth-giving Mother,*
> *You take us into the Womb of your Self*
> *and nurture us with your life's blood.*
> *Form us anew in Your own image:*
> *That, dying to the distortions of our past,*
> *We enter with joy into Your New Creation.*

> —MARY SCHMITT[3]

INVITATION TO REFLECT

Spend a while sitting still and focusing gently on your breathing, allowing yourself to become quiet inside. Then respond to these questions. You may find writing your answers in your journal helps you to engage more fully with the questions.

- What reaction do you have to the idea of being enwombed in God as a Birth Mother? Does this disturb or resonate with you in any way?

- What would it mean for you to "surrender to the Mother"?

- Does the invitation to be enwombed in God evoke in you any sense of deeper yearning? Express your response to God in whatever way is most expressive for you (for example through verbal prayer, art, poetry, dance, or music).

Now allow yourself to become quiet again, remaining still, open, and receptive to God for a few minutes.

NOTES

1. Quoted by Judson B. Trapnell in *Bede Griffiths: A Life in Dialogue* (Albany, NY: State University of New York Press, 2001), p. 9. To listen to Griffiths describe the experience he had, you can hear him here: https://www.youtube.com/watch?v=z3Dm6bt-sO0&t=206s.

2. From the title of Richard Rohr's book, *Everything Belongs: The Gift of Contemplative Prayer* (Chestnut Ridge, NY: Crossroad, 2003).

3. Mary Kathleen Speegle Schmitt, in *Seasons of the Feminine Divine: Christian Feminist Prayers for the Liturgical Cycle* (Chestnut Ridge, NY: Crossroad, 1993).

8

The Dance of Grace
and Participation

*"Is there anything I can do
to make myself Enlightened?"*

*"As little as you can do
to make the sun rise in the morning."*

*"Then of what use
are the spiritual exercises you prescribe?"*

*"To make sure you are not asleep
when the sun begins to rise."*

–ANTHONY DE MELLO[1]

When we embark on a deeper spiritual journey, we may wonder how much this process of inner transformation is the work of God and how much is up to us. Is it really necessary to engage in regular contemplative practices? Isn't transformation a work that's accomplished by the grace of God? And if that's the case, why do we need to play a part?

The story of Jesus calming the storm offers some answers to these questions.

> That day when evening came, he said to his disciples, "Let us go over to the other side." Leaving the crowd behind, they took him along, just as he was, in the boat. There were also other boats with him. A furious squall came up, and the waves broke over the boat, so that it was nearly swamped. Jesus was in the stern, sleeping on a cushion. The disciples woke him and said to him, "Teacher, don't you care if we drown?"
>
> He got up, rebuked the wind and said to the waves, "Quiet! Be still!" Then the wind died down and it was completely calm. He said to his disciples, "Why are you so afraid? Do you still have no faith?" (Mark 4:35–40)

Do you notice that Jesus seemed disappointed the disciples asked him to fix the situation? He asked them, "Do you still have no faith?" This seems a strange question, since they had just expressed their belief that he could help them. And yes, the story tells us he did help them, by calming the troubled waters, but he seemed reluctant.

In our own lives, when our lives and minds are troubled, we often cry out to God to fix the situation and ease our troubled minds. Sometimes we do receive a form of consolation, a calming of the waters of our turbulent thoughts, emotions, and circumstances. But as our spiritual lives deepen, ironically, this consolation tends to happen less and less. This can bring on a crisis of faith; we may become permanently disillusioned with prayer—or we may be driven still deeper in our faith journey.

Imagine being in a small boat in the midst of a tempest so wild that even experienced fishermen were terrified. Now picture Jesus asleep in your boat. The sleeping Jesus gives us a lovely picture of the deepest level of faith: rather than expecting God to fix our troubled lives or minds with a flick of the Divine wand, we join Jesus as he naps calmly amid the turbulence. This depth of faith isn't the result of a magical spell or some miraculous feat. It requires practice.

The Place of Contemplative Practice

Regular contemplative practice expands our maturity and steadies our hearts, to the point where we know nothing can shake us. This does not mean God is not working in us at the same time—the Spirit is continually guiding us—but this guidance is subtle and interior, requiring deep inner stillness and listening, the kind of listening the poet Rumi describes as making "everything in you an ear, each atom of your being."[2]

And so, as we grow deeper in faith, God's grace dances continually with our active participation, as Paul described in his letter to the Philippians:

> Continue to work out your salvation with fear and trembling; for it is God who is at work in you, both to will and to work for His good pleasure. (2:12)

The process of inner transformation continually interweaves God's grace with our participation. Our participation expresses our "yes" to God as we drop our barriers and allow God to work deep within us, transforming us from the inside out.

Some years ago, I went through something difficult and painful: a close friend was in the hospital (and ultimately died) from a serious injury that had happened when I was with her. During this time of crisis, I was amazed by the inner stability and peace I found in my prayer times, a sense of God's undergirding presence that carried me through everything. I realized how sturdy was the bedrock of trust God had developed in me over the previous few years. I believe this inner calm was a consequence of having taken my contemplative practices seriously in the time leading up to this incident. God's grace and my faithful daily practice had woven together to create a resilient strength of spirit.

God never imposes on us but works with our willingness to participate with us in our growth. This is the dance of grace and participation that mysteriously creates the process of inner transformation.

It is for God to grant grace;
your task is to accept that grace
and to guard it.

—SAINT CYRIL OF JERUSALEM[5]

INVITATION TO REFLECT

Spend a while sitting still and focusing gently on your breathing, allowing yourself to become quiet inside. Then reflect on these questions:

- What would it mean for you to "participate with all of your being" with what God is doing in your life through the turbulence of life-as-it-is?

- Are there any difficult areas of potential growth you know you have been resisting, where you sense an invitation to bring a "yes" to what God is doing? If you are able, express your "yes" now in whatever way is most meaningful for you.

Now allow yourself to become quiet again, remaining still, open, and receptive to God for a few minutes.

NOTES

1. Anthony de Mello. *One Minute Wisdom* (New York: Image, 1985), p. 10.

2. Andrew Harvey. *Light upon Light: Inspirations from Rumi* (Berkeley, CA: North Atlantic Books, 1996), p. 99.

3. Cyril of Jerusalem. *The Catechetical Lectures of S. Cyril, Archbishop of Jerusalem* (Oxford, UK: John Henry Parker, 1845), p. 12. Cyril was a fourth-century theologian who also served as the bishop of Jerusalem .

9

The Hidden Inner Work

As for everyone who comes to me
and hears my words
and puts them into practice,
I will show you what they are like.
They are like a person building a house,
who dug down deep and laid the foundation on rock.
When a flood came, the torrent struck that house
but could not shake it, because it was well built.
But the one who hears my words
and does not put them into practice
is like a man who built a house
on the ground without a foundation.
The moment the torrent struck that house,
it collapsed and its destruction was complete.

−LUKE 6:47-49

When we embark on a deeper spiritual journey, inner groundwork helps to ensure that any growth and transformation will be authentic, robust, and lasting. Jesus' wisdom teaching in these verses addresses the importance of laying these sturdy foundations. He encourages us to invest quietly and surely in the deeply grounded substructure that underpins our growth.

We spend so much time and energy worrying about the external structures of our lives: how well we are doing (in terms of finances or prestige), what people think of us, or whether we are doing what is expected. This is like a builder fussing over the prettiness of the house's siding and landscaping without ever bothering to pour cement for the foundation. The whole building would be in danger of imminent collapse.

This is often what is happening spiritually when people sink into holes of existential despair or severe depression: they have failed to develop the deep-grounded inner structures they need to support their exterior lives. These foundations are not visible from the outside, and they may not be glamorous work or satisfy any external criteria—yet when they are laid deeply and carefully, they ensure that whatever else is built on top will stand firm.

Hiddenness

The concept of hiddenness may be challenging to our ego-need to display our spiritual growth and value to society. The invitation, however, is to allow this inner work to unfold in secret, in obscurity, not looking for merit or praise, but trusting God with the outcome. As Paul wrote: "For you died, and your life is now hidden with Christ in God" (Colossians 3:3). Sometimes we even need to endure others' disapproval in order to stay true to our deepening faith journey. Ultimately, the choice to quietly follow the path we know is unfolding before us, to go deeper into the spiritual work to which we are being invited, strengthens that inner foundation.

I have accepted the challenge to let go of my worry about all the external stuff that occupies my thinking so much of the time. Instead, I keep returning my focus to the hidden inner work, laying my foundations deeply in God through regular contemplative practices. Some notes I penned during a silent retreat reflect this:

> It strikes me how little I have noticed the many voices I have allowed to control me from out there, how much I have allowed myself to be plucked around by expectations, or by my outer projections. I have allowed myself to become imprisoned by these. The key is to attend more and more to the hidden foundations, to go deeper into the freedom of God.

I also penned this note to self, from the same retreat: "Keep working on the foundations, the hidden inner work, and no matter what happens in the outer world, the structure will remain standing."

Withdrawing from the Social Game

Another wisdom teaching from Jesus is found in his counsel about prayer:

> And when you pray, do not be like the hypocrites, for they love to pray standing in the synagogues and on the street corners to be seen by others. Truly I tell you, they have received their reward in full. But when you pray, go into your inner room, close the door and pray to your Father, who is unseen. Then your Father, who sees what is done in secret, will reward you. (Matthew 6:5–6)

In theologian James Alison's comments on this passage,[1] he noted that we like to think of ourselves as independent free thinkers, especially in the West, where personal freedom is one of the values we strongly defend. But he went on to say that we don't recognize the extent to which we are social beings, shaped by the people around us and the subculture in which we grew up.

This tendency dominates many churches, creating templates of how you should look and act if you are a good Anglican / Catholic / charismatic / father figure / supportive wife / social justice advocate (and so on, depending on the focus of the subculture). We so easily adapt ourselves to these stereotypes without even being aware of what we are doing. More broadly, in our consumerist society, marketing depends on the need we have to fit in socially, and the advertising business is remarkably effective at making us want what we never knew we wanted! This is called mimetic theory, which in a nutshell says that we desire what others desire, so that we are basically copying each other's desires.

As humans, we have an incredibly strong need for the approval of others. As a result, we are far from free. Just watch your thoughts for a while, and you'll notice how much of your behavior is tailored to create a good impression.

We float through life, propelled by the currents of this sea of others' positive or negative regard. Even if we fight against complying with others' expectations, rebellion itself can become a different sort of trap. Whether we comply or rebel, our responses are conditioned by the society around us; we either seek to win approval or we react against it. Neither of these is a free response. Both options turn us into puppets that dance to strange tunes, instead of being able to operate freely from our authentic inner selves.

In the passage from the Gospel of Matthew at the beginning of this chapter, Jesus tells us that those who engage in outward displays of piety can expect only the reward they are seeking: others' approval and admiration. However, public opinion is fickle. Instead of boosting our sense of self, dependence on others' affirmation actually erodes our identities. As we hungrily lap up attention, believing our identities depend on it, we become addicted to this rewards system—and we become trapped in behaviors we hope will keep our "approval ratings" up. Social success can make us feel hollow inside, because the rewards are always superficial and short-lived, creating anxiety and insecurity. It fortifies the outer persona, not the inner core identity. When we receive blame instead of the praise we desperately crave, the consequences can be devastating. Our lives are lived at the end of a cruel whip, craving the highs and terrified of the lows.

In his teaching about prayer, Jesus suggests an alternative: regularly withdraw from this game, letting go of the outer need for approval by shutting the door on it completely. As we disidentify with any outer descriptors of who we are, we can move inward to where we hear the approval of God.

Shutting the Inner Door

In Matthew 6, Jesus tells us to seek out private, secret places where we can enter into relationship with God. This is a much more solid and consistent Source for our identities. Supported by this generous Presence, the Ground of our being, we become more and more rooted in the unshakable inner identity of who we are in God. Again, this is inner work done in secret, but it builds a firm foundation that can withstand any turbulence.

And life is unavoidably turbulent. Eckhart Tolle said he can summarize the theme of every movie in three words: "Something Goes Wrong."[2] That is the nature of life. When we know who we are at a deeper level, however, our well-being no longer depends on life going "right" (or how we want it to).

As we grow in this inner sense of identity, we discover a much deeper joy, freedom, and satisfaction than we ever receive from outer approval. However, to be rooted in the inner self requires a conscious letting go of the outer persona. It's not that we withdraw permanently from "normal life," but rather that we choose to *not believe* or identify with the external stories about who we are, whether good or bad. Instead, we take regular time out to hear God's story of who we are, which is so much more creative, deeply rooted, and secure. As Eckhart Tolle said, "Deriving my identity from my successes or reputation is a cheap substitute for who I really am."[3]

The Freedom of the Inner Private Room

When Jesus spoke about a "private room," he wasn't referring to an actual room in a house, since in his day, peoples' homes had few, if any, private spaces. Every room was intended for communal use. So Jesus was talking about a metaphorical space within us, a space of psychological and spiritual withdrawal from the outer game of public reward. The Greek word used here referred to a storehouse or a pantry, a room that was completely shut off from the outer world in order to keep the temperature constant.

This describes the inner space into which Jesus invites us. As we shut out the outside voices, we are freed from the anxiety and tension we experience in the sea of other people's regard. We enter a place that is calm and stable, where all that turbulence is kept out. There, in that secret state of solitude, our identities and our sense of "okayness" are stable, grounded in the quiet confidence of God's vision of who we are.

We need to revisit this place frequently. Only when we are operating from this space are we truly free, not dancing like a puppet to others' tunes by either trying to win their approval or reacting to their disapproval. As we return regularly to this peaceful metaphorical pantry, our core identities become rooted more and more deeply in God. Then, this inner confidence generates our outer behaviors; we act from this place where we know who we are. Without good "pantry time," though, we are in danger of getting trapped once more in the web of people's desires. When that happens, we become part of the problem, contributing to the outer sea of turbulence.

Henri Nouwen wrote:

> Your true identity is as a child of God. This is the identity you have to accept. Once you have claimed it and settled in it, you can live in a world that gives you much joy as well as pain . . . , because the identity that makes you free is anchored beyond all human praise and blame.[4]

In our daily times of contemplative practice, we return to this place of freedom. When we enter this inner room—the quiet, temperature-controlled pantry that's protected from the fluctuations and noisy demands of the outside world—we let go of all the voices that praise and criticize us. The quiet gives us a break from our knee-jerk reactions to these voices, and we have space to disconnect from the identities that are linked with outward performance. We relax into being ourselves with God, who not only loves us but who also *likes* us. The Life-Giver longs for us to discover the freedom of resting in unconditional Divine approval.

Those of us who have been involved in contemplative practice for a while know it's not enough to merely choose to be by ourselves, shutting a physical door on the outside world. Our minds are one of the most treacherous parts of the praise-blame system; they not only amplify and rehash others' voices, but they also project negative opinions onto others, imagining criticisms we never actually heard. Our minds can be our worst torturers.

That's why we need practices that allow us to deal with this inner noise, so we are able to recognize and let go of persistent and destructive thought patterns. Regular practice will lay down new pathways in our neural networks, training our minds to let go of the entangled system that so easily entraps us. With daily repetition, we form new habits of constantly returning to the simple freedom of being present, open, and awake to the One who is always already present.

> *The temptation [is] to disconnect*
> *from that deep place in you where God dwells*
> *and to let yourself be drowned*
> *in the praise or blame of the world. . . .*
> *Only God can fully dwell*
> *in that deepest place in you*

and give you a sense of safety.
There lies your true freedom.

—HENRI NOUWEN[5]

INVITATION TO REFLECT

Spend a while sitting still and focusing gently on your breathing, allowing yourself to become quiet inside. Then take some time to reflect on your answers to these questions, writing in your journal if that helps you to stay focused.

- In what ways do you get caught in the praise or blame of others? When do you feel as if you are reacting to people or circumstances, rather than responding from a free place within?

- What would it mean for you to withdraw from the praise / blame system of the outer world? In what practical ways might you find freedom from this?

- Do you have a sense of what it means, at this point in your life, to focus more on the hidden inner work? Reflect on what is possible for you within the constraints of your everyday life.

Now allow yourself to become quiet again, remaining still, open, and receptive to God for a few more minutes.

NOTES

1. James Alison. "Prayer: A Case Study in Mimetic Anthropology" in *Jesus the Forgiving Victim: Listening for the Unheard Voice* (Glenview, IL: Doers Publishing, 2013).

2. Eckhart Tolle. *Talks at Google: Eckhart Tolle in Conversation with Bradley Horowitz*, available at https://www.youtube.com/watch?v=qE1dWwoJPU0.

3. Ibid.

4. Henri J. M. Nouwen. *The Inner Voice of Love: A Journey Through Anguish to Freedom* (New York: Image Books, 2010), p. 70.

5. Ibid.

PART III

Becoming Still

10

Silent Prayer

Then Jacob awoke from his sleep and said,
"Surely the Lord is in this place, and I did not know it.
. . . How awesome is this place!
This is none other than the house of God,
and this is the gate of heaven."

−GENESIS 28:16-17

The gate of heaven is everywhere.

−THOMAS MERTON[1]

Picture a child sitting on her parent's lap while watching a scary movie. The child is totally engrossed in the movie, to the point of forgetting that she is safely held in her parent's arms. The movie is so absorbing and frightening that the child feels terrified and threatened. Only when the child is reminded of where she actually is, bringing her awareness back to her body and the immediacy of where she is sitting safely on her parent's lap, does she realize the movie is just a fictional story. There is nothing to fear.

This is how we perceive life. We are like children caught in the garish drama of a movie. Our minds are constantly interpreting life to us, imagining a whole world of possibility, regurgitating the past, anticipating the future, and of course we place ourselves always at the center of these dramas. Because we are so caught up in these stories, we are not aware of the reality of what David Frennette describes as the presence of God that "silently, secretly holds you throughout your whole life."[2] We are also not able to truly hold other people's interests at heart, because our perspectives are so distorted and self-interested.

The Internal Cinema Screen of Our Minds

Most of what we see on our mental cinema screens has never happened, nor will it *ever* happen—or if it does, our interpretations of events are highly distorted. I'm not saying that suffering does not happen; of course, suffering is very real in our lives, but more often than not, we create additional suffering through our thoughts and imaginations. As we saw in chapter 4, neurobiological research has found that our minds cling to negative experiences, causing our brains to be shaped by them, while positive experiences slip off our minds. This means we mainly remember harsh, negative, or fearful experiences. Rick Hanson, a neurobiologist who specializes in this area, noted that "acquiring a big pile of negative experiences in implicit memory banks naturally makes a person more anxious, irritable, and blue. Plus it makes it harder to be patient and giving toward others."[3]

I've noticed that my mind amplifies anything to do with conflict, disharmony, or the possibility that somebody is displeased with me, turning it into my primary sense of reality. Any slight evidence that someone is unhappy with me is fed into my internal amplifier, where it is dialed up to scary levels, creating an entire imagined drama in my mind. Although this drama is invariably untrue, its felt effects are very real, reinforcing my skewed perceptions.

This process goes on in most of our lives, getting worse with age if the cycle is not stopped. As a result, the continual negative, self-reinforcing drama replays in our heads all the time. The worst part of it is—we don't even know it. We think our minds' representations *are* reality, that they truly *are* the shape of our lives. We are caught in a nightmare, unable to realize that all we have to do to make the nightmare disappear is *wake up*.

This waking up is easier said than done. In our Western culture, we've become so mind-dominated that we can barely conceive of any way of being or connecting with God that doesn't involve our thoughts. Richard Rohr pointed out that our society's greatest addiction is not to alcohol or drugs or even food but to our habitual ways of thinking.[4] Most of our thoughts are trivial and repetitious. We like to think we control our minds, but mostly, our minds control us. We get stuck in patterns of thinking, and our minds are like a hamster running on a wheel, spinning around the same old thought processes.

Thomas Merton wrote, "Our minds are like crows. They pick up everything that glitters, no matter how uncomfortable our nests get with all that metal in them."[5] Our minds' obsession with busyness, commentaries, and stimulation creates uncomfortable and crowded inner spaces.

A key way to cut through the mind's incessant busyness is to learn new mental habits that recognize our thought streams, let them go, and return to the present moment. This immediately anchors us back in reality and breaks the thought pattern in which the mind was stuck. I find that the more I practice this, the easier it becomes to let go of my mind's obsessions. I have learned to take myself a lot less seriously, and I've felt less plagued by my old obsessive patterns.

Centering Prayer

The practice of silent prayer or meditation is, in my own experience, one of the most foundational contemplative practices. The method I use is Centering Prayer, described in the exercise at the end of this chapter. Here's how Father Thomas Keating described the work of Centering Prayer:

> Centering prayer is not so much the absence of thoughts as detachment from them. It is the opening of mind

and heart, body and emotions—our whole being—to God, the Ultimate Mystery, beyond words, thoughts, and emotions—beyond, in other words, the psychological content of the present moment. In centering prayer we do not deny or repress what is in our (conscious thinking process). We simply accept the fact of whatever is there and go beyond it, not by effort, but by letting go of whatever is there.[6]

Centering Prayer requires a choice, over and over again, to let go of thoughts, images, and distractions, continually returning in openhearted surrender to the presence of God. I have found this enables me to clear my inner space of clutter—all of the negative images and perceptions of the world that crowd my ordinary awareness. In Centering Prayer, I also open myself to God's presence and to the working of God's grace deep within me. As I let go of my own version of life, this opens me to the more spacious, loving, and generous sense of life that is already the truth. I just have to wake up to it.

On one of my retreats, I dreamed I was walking around a beautiful house that had just been built. It was perfectly finished, with smooth chrome accessories and clean lines, and everything worked perfectly. I used the toilet in the perfect bathroom, but when I flushed it, all sorts of rotten-looking stuff oozed out of the cistern. When I opened up the cistern, I found it was a mess of sewage, but it also had things I recognized, like the carrots from my garden I had previously cooked and eaten, and the stew I had cooked them in. I was embarrassed by the regurgitation of things from my life, this vile ugliness in the otherwise perfect house, and I panicked. How could I ever get rid of the mess? When I called the owner of the house, though, the owner quickly recognized the problem and said, "The solution is simple. The pipe with the water going in has been switched with the outflow pipe, and we just need to swap them back. Then it will work perfectly."

This dream's easy resolution to what had felt like a complex, messy situation lingered with me. What struck me most was the understanding that I merely needed to allow fresh water to flow into the system—rather than reintroducing all the waste that should be let out—and the whole system will be cleared.

This sounds laughably obvious in the case of a toilet, and yet we do this all the time with our minds. We allow our outlets to feed back in as the inlets, which leads to all manner of clogged-up mess and unhappiness. Any train of thought that is self-reinforcing, focused on our egos (even if our thoughts seem selfless, righteous, or virtuous), is the sewage we allow to flow in. Anything that bolsters our self-image—whether it is about doing "good" or being powerful or successful—feeds us unhealthy, regurgitated material that will rot us from inside. Judgmental or critical thoughts also add to the mess.

To reverse the flow, allowing fresh clean water to replace the polluted liquids of my ego, I've found I need to daily practice Centering Prayer. When I don't, I feel myself becoming murky inside. The dramas that go on in my head are oh-so convincing, like sticky substances that cling to my inner being. I am drawn to them, like a child to a colorful TV show. But when I continually make the choice to let go and return to the present moment, I can step out of the thought patterns that trap me. Gradually, I am becoming free of the negative power of their grip.

When we first begin this practice, though, it often seems as if nothing is happening. Many people give up in boredom, or they question the validity of this practice as a means of relating to God. The feelings of boredom or purposelessness arise because our minds are so used to the hyperstimulation of our dramas, our entertainment fixes, our beloved theories of God and life, our judgments and opinions, and all the other mental fantasies that go on in our minds all the time. With the regular practice of Centering Prayer, however, where we let go again and again of our internal dramas, we find that our thought addiction eases. The negative and narrow dramas we mistook for reality fade, and a fresh and freeing spaciousness opens within us.

Cynthia Bourgeault described this work:

If you wish to experience what lies beneath [ordinary thinking], spiritual tradition teaches, the first step is simply to pull the plug on that constant self-reflexive activity of the mind. And that's what intentional silence, or meditation, is set up to do. It's like putting a stick in the spoke of thinking, so that the whole closed circuit gets derailed and the more subtle awareness at the depths

of your being can begin to make its presence known.
. . . Meditation rests on the wager that if you can simply
break the tyranny of your ordinary awareness, the rest
will begin to unfold itself.[7]

As our awareness of the mind's habits and misinterpretations grows, we start to see a bigger picture. As a result, we feel less threatened by life, and we develop an increased capacity to welcome and stay with what is actually happening. Since we are not as caught up in our own interests and self-absorbed dramas as we used to be, we become more generous and sensitive to others' needs. Our capacity for compassion increases—toward our own stuck, broken selves, as well as toward others in their humanity and brokenness. We begin to experience a deep rootedness in God's presence, not so much as a clear image or personal presence but as a silent, secret holding by our Divine Parent.

This is a very subtle awareness, which is why at first it feels like nothing, especially compared to the lurid dramas that play in our heads. The awareness grows with practice, however, until it gradually becomes a defined pattern within our inner beings. As it shapes our way of knowing and perceiving reality, it opens new pathways for creative, compassionate, and life-giving responses.

When we wake up from the nightmare dramas of our internal cinema screens, we become more aware that every moment is filled with sacredness, and that God is here, now, with no condition and no exception.

What is so invasive
about all these stressors that we all go through
is this perception that we are nothing but these things,
that they have the power to name who we are.
But if in deep meditation
I can intimately experience a oneness with God
that transcends all these things,
that's the peace that surpasses understanding.
I know that yes, I face these things today,
these things are going on,
but the taproot of my heart is grounded
in the oneness that's not reducible
to any of these things.
And I think as people learn
to habituate that awareness,
it does transform their life.

—JAMES FINLEY[8]

INVITATION TO PRACTICE

Here are guidelines for the Centering Prayer method[9]:

- Choose a sacred word as the symbol of your intention to consent to God's presence and action within you.

- Sitting comfortably and with eyes closed, settle briefly and silently introduce the sacred word as the symbol of your consent to God's presence and action within you.

- When you notice yourself engaged with your thoughts (including body sensations, feelings, images, and reflections), return ever so gently to the sacred word.

- At the end of the prayer period, remain in silence with eyes closed for a couple of minutes.

As you practice this, don't judge yourself if your mind wanders. Be patient and compassionate with yourself whenever you notice you have been lost in thoughts.

Father Thomas Keating, who was instrumental in introducing the Centering Prayer method, recommended practicing for twenty minutes twice a day. If you struggle to make that kind of commitment, you might want to start with ten minutes a day and increase as you go. The most important thing to do is to develop a regular practice, so you can gradually disidentify from all the habitual mental processes and self-constructed identities that have become so sticky in your mind.

NOTES

1. Thomas Merton. *Conjectures of a Guilty Bystander* (New York: Image Books, 1966), p. 146.

2. David Frennette. *The Path of Centering Prayer: Deepening Your Experience of God* (Boulder, CO: Sounds True, 2017), p. 57.

3. Rick Hanson, "Take in the Good" from his blog at http://www.rickhanson.net/take-in-the-good/.

4. Richard Rohr. "A Vital Spiritual Experience" from his Daily Meditations, November 17, 2015, https://cac.org/daily-meditations/.

5. Thomas Merton. *New Seeds of Contemplation* (New York: New Directions, 2007), p. 104.

6. Thomas Keating. *Open Mind, Open Heart: The Contemplative Dimension of the Gospel* (New York: Continuum, 1995), p. 12.

7. Cynthia Bourgeault, *Centering Prayer and Inner Awakening* (Cambridge, MA: Cowley Publications, 2004), p. 16.

8. James Finley. From an interview "Experiencing God Through Meditation," *Beliefnet,* https://www.beliefnet.com/faiths/prayer/experiencing-god-through-meditation.aspx.

9. *The Method of Centering Prayer* brochure, Contemplative Outreach Ltd., 2016. More details of this method can be read in the brochure, available at https://www.contemplativeoutreach.org/sites/default/files/private/methodcpeng-2016-060.pdf.

11

Inner Listening

Make everything in you an ear,
each atom of your being,
and you will hear at every moment
what the Source is whispering to you,
just to you and for you,
without any need for my words or anyone else's.
You are—we all are—the beloved of the Beloved,
and in every moment, in every event of your life,
the Beloved is whispering to you
exactly what you need to hear and know.
Who can ever explain this miracle? It simply is.
Listen and you will discover it every passing moment.
Listen, and your whole life
will become a conversation in thought and act
between you and the Beloved,
directly, wordlessly, now and always.

—RUMI[1]

L istening to God—which we can also refer to as *inner knowing*—is a practice that teaches us to attune to a wise, quiet voice rising from the secret place where God dwells in the depths of our being. This inner wisdom is what Jesus described as the work of the Holy Spirit: the Counselor, the Comforter, and the Spirit of Truth (John 15:26). Llewellyn Vaughan-Lee spoke of this as an inner listening for the voice of the Beloved:

> He [sic] often doesn't speak in a loud voice, He doesn't always come banging on the door. Often He speaks very quietly. He whispers to you about the secrets of your own soul, and the secrets of Love. It's very beautiful when you are told in your heart about those secrets, and you hear them. But you have to learn to listen, and that means learning to still the mind, learning to put away all of those everyday thoughts. This is one of the first steps in meditation. You create inward space within your heart, within your mind, where you can be with God, where you can listen to God. It can be done.[2]

This inner knowing or listening is much deeper than our typical mental activities. Less "intellectual," it has a more body-grounded quality to it. We are not used to operating at this level. Our thoughts are the only kind of *knowing* with which we are familiar.

John Prendergast described inner knowing as "the still, small voice."

It's a very quiet knowing that's different from the conditioned mind. It's a different quality of knowing, it's much quieter, it doesn't explain itself, it doesn't rationalize itself, and yet it's authoritative. We don't often hear it in words as much as have it as a felt sense in our body. It can relate to very practical matters, decisions that we are making in ordinary life, but it also can guide us in terms of our understanding of our depths, in terms of our psychological process, and our feelings, in terms of getting in touch with what we are actually experiencing, and even more deeply it is our way of knowing ourselves most intimately. It's our inner authority, or our inner teacher.[3]

This deeper kind of knowing requires inner quiet, so that our spiritual awareness can begin to attune to the still, small voice.

The ancient Greek name for the voice of wisdom is *Sophia*, who is the feminine figure in the Book of Proverbs that embodies the wisdom of God. Joyce Rupp wrote:

> Sophia is your true self's best friend. She is a voice in the dark, a whisper of calm and courage amid the ego's strong voice of fear and clinging to security. As the ego fights to have its way, Sophia keeps moving the true self to the open window, offering clarity, insight and vision. It is Sophia who gifts us with inner freedom.[4]

The Requirements of Inner Listening

Silence, solitude, intention, presence, surrender, and time are the
necessary ingredients of inner listening.

> *Silence:* We need to separate ourselves from the usual
> noisy voices and emotions that take up so much space
> in our heads.

> *Solitude:* When we close the door of our inner rooms,
> shutting out external distractions for a while, we are more
> free to enter this space of deep knowing.

> *Intention:* Bringing intention to our listening creates the
> conditions of poised openness and readiness that allow
> us to be receptive to the still, small voice.

> *Presence:* Only when we are present to the here and now,
> will we experience the presence of the I AM. We need
> this proximity to the Divine to hear at a deeper level.
> Being present allows us to enter a deeper space than the
> typical mind-level of knowing, and in this space, we can
> hear the deeper stirrings of the Spirit, the knowing of
> our True Selves.

> *Surrender:* When we let go of our own wills and our need
> to control our lives, we open to a greater wisdom that will

always be more creative, life-giving, and fresh than our own ideas of how reality should be.

Time: It takes us a while to quieten down and let our busy minds settle, so we have to allow time in silence, solitude, and presence to hear the quiet voice emerging from our inner depths.

Qualities of the Inner Voice

This inner knowing we are exploring is not a knowing *about* God or life or anything else our minds can get hold of. It is not intellectual *knowledge* but rather an awareness grounded in the body.

This awareness doesn't happen instantaneously; we slowly grow into it with daily practice. Then, when we are spiritually attuned, we often don't "hear" anything precise or obvious. Instead, we may experience a sensation in our physical gut. Through Centering Prayer, I have gradually come to *know* God's unconditional love. This consciousness is organically rooted in me at a level much deeper than any knowledge I could put into words; across my solar plexus, I have a perception of deep-fixed peace and stability, no matter what my physical or emotional circumstances are. Often, an unexpected smile arises from within me, cutting through my self-absorbed crankiness.

Sometimes, a "hearing" can bubble up to the surface, where our minds catch some threads that arise from our depths. When that happens, we need to distinguish the still, small voice from our own mental projections. Knowing some of the characteristics of the inner voice can help us with that discernment.

One of the qualities of the Divine voice is that it is soft and calm, subtle and undemanding. It is so quiet that our own inner noise can easily drown it out. That is why we need to enter a silent inner space.

Another quality of God's voice is that it offers fresh and creative insights. It cuts through our usual thought processes and breaks out of our habitual mental boxes to come up with new ideas or perspectives that never occurred to us before. I've found inner listening gives me a sense of possibility, the awareness that life is filled with previously unsuspected potential. I often have an "aha!" moment: first, I notice my own silliness, and then, as the Spirit breathes life and hope into the stale areas of my life, a feeling of empowerment blossoms within me, assuring me there is a way out of my stuckness.

God's voice is also affirming. Many of us expect to hear God pointing out our failures and weaknesses, constantly correcting us. As a result, we often put harsh and judgmental words into God's mouth. But when we read the mystics, people who have devoted most of their lives to being quiet and listening to God, we learn something different. These mystics talk about God's voice as that of a gentle, tender parent or a passionate, attentive lover. As Richard Rohr wrote:

Those who enter deeply into the great mystery do not experience a God who compares, differentiates, and judges. They experience an all-embracing receptor, a receiver who looks at the divine image in us and almost refuses to look at the contrary.[5]

I have realized that God's voice is *never* harsh or grating. The Beloved will never judge or condemn us. In fact, I believe if we ever hear anything judgmental, harsh, or belittling, it is our own projection of what we expect God to be saying.

Scott Anstadt, a clinical social worker and spiritual teacher, explained this tendency we have to project our insecurities onto God:

In virtually every circumstance leading us to feelings of discomfort, we have placed our attention upon ego fears. All fears can be reduced to one core illusion, the illusion that we are alone and not worthy of God (because of our guilt over this or that). . . . There is nothing we can do to be judged as undeserving of the love of God.[6]

As time goes by and we become more and more familiar with the qualities of this subtle stirring, this gentle voice, we will be able to access it more readily in our daily lives. Then we will be able to draw from the inner well of wisdom wherever we are, whatever we are doing.

God's wisdom is something mysterious
that goes deep into the interior of his purposes.
You don't find it lying around on the surface.
It's not the latest message, but more like the oldest—
what God determined as the way to bring out his best in us.
. . . The Spirit, not content to flit around on the surface,
dives into the depths of God,
and brings out what God planned all along. . . .
Spirit can be known only by spirit—
God's Spirit and our spirits in open communion.
Spiritually alive, we have access to everything God's Spirit is doing.

–1 Corinthians 2:7-15

INVITATION TO PRACTICE

Lectio Divina—sacred reading—is a way of hearing God through scripture or other sacred or inspirational writing, with the emphasis on hearing with our hearts rather than analyzing the text with our minds.[7]

Lectio Divina consists of four movements:

I. Lectio (reading): Find a comfortable position where you can remain alert and yet also relax your body. Bring your attention to your breath and allow a few moments to become centered. If you find yourself distracted at any time, gently return to the rhythm of your breath as an anchor for your awareness. Settle into this moment and become fully present.

Then read the passage once or twice through slowly and listen for a word or phrase that feels significant right now, that captures your attention even if you don't know why. Gently repeat this word or phrase to yourself in the silence.

2. Meditatio (reflection): Read the text again, and then allow the word or phrase that caught your attention in the first movement to spark your imagination. Savor the word or phrase with all your senses; notice what smells, sounds, tastes, sights, and feelings are evoked. Then listen for what images, feelings, and memories are stirring, welcoming them in and then savoring this experience and resting in it.

3. Oratio (prayer response): Read the text a third time, and then listen for how it might link with your everyday life. Is there an invitation? A nudging toward a new awareness or action? Allow prayer to arise spontaneously in response to your heart being touched by God.

4. Contemplatio (resting in contemplation): Move into a time for simply resting in God, allowing your heart to fill with gratitude for God's presence in this time of prayer. Slow your thoughts and reflections even further and sink into the experience of stillness. Rest in the presence of God, and allow yourself to simply be.

Finally, gently connect with your breath again and slowly bring your awareness back to the room, moving from inner experience to outer experience. Give yourself some time of transition between these moments of contemplative depth and your everyday life.

NOTES

1. Adapted from Andrew Harvey's *Light upon Light: Inspirations from Rumi* (Berkeley, CA: North Atlantic Books, 1996), p. 99.

2. Llewellyn Vaughan-Lee, from the talk "Where the Two Seas Meet: Meditation," transcript of talk given December 13, 2009 in Tiburon, California, available online at https://www.goldensufi.org/a_medita-tion_talk_transcript.html.

3. John J. Prendergast in an interview with Tami Simon, "The Deep Heart," *Insights at the Edge* (Sounds True, December 23, 2019), available at https://www.stitcher.com/show/insights-at-the-edge/episode/john-j-prendergast-the-deep-heart-65910240.

4. Joyce Rupp. *The Star in My Heart: Experiencing Sophia, Inner Wisdom* (Notre Dame, IN: Ave Maria Press, 2003), (no page number available).

5. Richard Rohr. *Everything Belongs: The Gift of Contemplative Prayer* (Chestnut Ridge, NY: Crossroad, 2003), p. 66.

6. Scott Anstadt. "Opening the Door of Communication to the Voice of Our Spiritual Power," *Inner Self,* https://innerself.com/.

7. Adapted from Christine Valter Paintner's *Lectio Divina: The Sacred Art* (London, UK: SPCK Publishing, 2011).

12

Presence

The spiritual life
can only be lived in the present moment, in the now.
All the great religious traditions insist upon
this simple but difficult truth.
When we go rushing ahead into the future,
or sinking back into the past,
we miss the hand of God,
which can only touch us in the now.

—CYNTHIA BOURGEAULT[1]

If we want to go deeper in our spiritual lives, we need to practice being present to each moment. All too often, we are lost in our thoughts rather than aware of the *now* that surrounds us.

We do not need to physically retreat from the world to practice this form of contemplation. As Buddhist teacher Dipa Ma wrote:

If you are busy, then busyness is the meditation. Meditation is to know what you are doing. . . . If you are rushing to the office, then you should be mindful of "rushing." When you are eating, putting on your shoes, your socks, your clothes, you must be mindful. It is all meditation![2]

Mindfulness

Mark Williams, a professor at Oxford University who contributed to the development of a branch of psychotherapy called mindfulness-based cognitive therapy, describes mindfulness in this way:

Mindfulness is . . . a direct, intuitive knowing of what you are doing while you are doing it. Most of the time our attention is hijacked by our thoughts and emotions, by our concerns, by our worries for the future, and our regrets and memories of the past. Mindful awareness is about learning to pay attention, in the present moment, and without judgment. It's like training a muscle—training attention to be where you want it to be . . . allowing us to choose how we respond and react.[3]

Mindfulness is the choice to live in the present moment as fully as possible, without sorting circumstances into "good" and "bad" categories. We bring our attention into whatever we are doing, knowing we are doing it, rather than operating on autopilot. We use our senses to pay attention and to truly experience where we are and what we are doing—smelling and tasting our food, feeling the ground underneath our feet as we walk or the chair underneath us as we sit, and noticing the sounds we hear, rather than letting them get lost in the background. When we do this, we are immediately brought back to the present, and in that moment, we are free from the drama going on in our minds.

The focus in mindfulness is on the present moment, not the past or the future. One of the strange characteristics of our minds is that they are hardly ever in the here and now; they are always chewing over the past, anxious about the future, or obsessing about what is happening elsewhere. But neither the past nor the future actually exists, except as fantasies in our minds—and we cannot change what happened in the past or even what will happen in the future. All we can do is attend to the here and now as fully as possible, because this is all that exists.

The Message paraphrase of Jesus' words puts this beautifully:

Give your entire attention to what God is doing right now, and don't get worked up about what may or may not happen tomorrow. God will help you deal with whatever hard things come up when the time comes. (Matthew 6:34)

Practicing this requires an ongoing choice to let go of our mind-chatter and return to the present moment, paying attention to what is in the here and now, whatever the content of it may be. Thich Nhat Hanh had a saying he encouraged his readers to repeat often: "Present moment, wonderful moment."[4]

Brother Lawrence was a seventeenth-century Carmelite monk who practiced this awareness as he worked in the monastery kitchen. He did everything, even peeling potatoes, as a sacred act. "If I so much as pick up something that's dropped on the ground," he said, "I find joy in doing it for God."[5] He called this *practicing the presence of God.*

Brother Lawrence faced the same challenges we do when we try to practice mindfulness. He wrote:

> My thoughts are the biggest obstacles to this way of living my life. The little useless thoughts that drift through my head, making mischief, distracting me. I've learned to reject them as soon as I notice them. They have nothing to do with the reality at hand—nor with my eternal salvation—and once I stop paying attention to them, I can get back to communing with God.[6]

Mindfulness asks that we be present to our physical experience of the world (our senses), as well as our own thoughts and our emotions. As we do this, we attune ourselves to the subtle awareness that God holds us through all life's moments.

Thomas Merton wrote in one of his later journals:

The grip the *present* has on me. This is the one thing that has grown most noticeably in my spiritual life—nothing much else has. The rest dims, as it should. I am getting older. The reality of now—the unreality of all the rest. The unreality of ideas and explanations and formulas. I am.[7]

On my silent retreats, I am always amazed by how powerfully the practice of being mindful, truly aware of each moment, opens me to the presence and mystery of God. At the same time, I am appalled at how little I manage to practice this in my daily life. All too often, I allow my busyness to run roughshod over the quiet, tender, and undemanding call to simply *be*. I am challenged to bring greater intention and discipline to the practice of presence.

Over the past few years, I have been paying attention to my mind's activity, and it has been an interesting but also alarming journey of discovery. One of the things I've noticed is how repetitive and unhelpful my thoughts are. Even worse than that, I see how poisonous my mind can be. It drip-feeds my painful emotions with unhelpful self-speak; it creates a continual, warped commentary on life, usually with me as the poor, misunderstood victim. All this keeps me stuck in unhappy patterns of thought and cramped emotions. On one of my retreats, when I recognized what my mind had been up to, I wrote in my journal: "I've been worshipping too much at the church of the poison mind!"

I've come to understand that any perception I have that life is unmanageable, withholding, or threatening is just that — a perception. As Anthony de Mello wrote:

> Think of somebody you are living with or working with whom you do not like, who causes negative feelings to arise in you. . . . The first thing you need to understand is that the negative feeling is inside you. You are responsible for the negative feeling, not the other person.[8]

In other words, when we get upset with someone, we are actually believing and allowing ourselves to be oppressed by a story our minds have spun. Richard Rohr, in one of his daily meditations, said something similar: "I don't have the idea; the idea has me. I don't have the feeling; the feeling has me."[9] And Cynthia Bourgeault explained:

> It is not a matter of replacing negative emotions with positive emotions. . . . You do not have to make the terror or anger or grief go way; you simply have to hunker down . . . and allow the surface of life to be as its it. Amazingly, you discover that at the depths, Being still holds firm.[10]

When I consider the way my thoughts trap me, I imagine myself inside a wild thicket with multiple layers of entangled, thorny branches. Escaping is no simple matter—and meanwhile, this snarl of briars is the impetus that drives many of my actions. As a result, much of my life is an automatic reaction driven by guilt, fear, craving, resisting, defending, or needing to be liked or approved.

Nearly eight billion of us are all reacting out of these same negative motivations, all feeding into each other's turbulent sea of reaction and feedback. No wonder the world is such a mess!

The Renewing of Our Minds

The apostle Paul wrote:

> Do not conform to the pattern of this world, but be transformed by the renewing of your mind. Then you will be able to test and approve what God's will is—his good, pleasing and perfect will. (Romans 12:2)

This passage points to how inner transformation and freedom take place—by the renewing of our minds. A modern analogy would be hitting the reset button on a computer. When a computer functions more and more slowly, rebooting the computer will clear the RAM memory of all the bits and pieces of information that have been clogging and bloating the system. Restarting the computer allows it to begin afresh with a clean memory. This is what we desperately need to learn for ourselves: to hit a reset button in our minds, wiping the memory clean so we can begin again.

One way we do this is by consciously and intentionally detaching ourselves from the thorny tangle in our heads and returning to the present, here and now, to our breathing, to how our bodies are feeling or doing. This immediately anchors us back in reality and breaks the thought pattern that had ensnared the mind. I have found that the more I practice this, the more easily I can let go of the mind's obsessions, allowing me to take myself a lot less seriously. My mind's obsessive patterns lose their grasp on me.

Presence is crucial if we want to move into the deeper dimensions of our spiritual journeys. Being in the present moment, here and now, is the only place and time we can find God, the I AM, the Present One.

Whenever I do become present, I realize the extent to which I have been living in a world of make-believe in my head. On one of my retreats, I wrote this in my journal:

> My mind is constantly creating stories about everything! And then I believe that is reality. Only by being present am I actually in the place where God is, because God is BEING. God is not a story. God is not a concept. God is not in the future or past. Those are all stories. God is I AM.

We fall back into autopilot mode so easily. Brother Lawrence admitted he too had a tendency to return to his old thought patterns—but then he advised, "Don't worry about it, since worry will only distract you further. Bring yourself back to silence, to tranquility."[11] When we fall back asleep, sinking down into the old numbing and nonproductive thoughts, we always have the option to wake up again. As we return to simply being present, we once more feel relief from the oppressive thoughts that plague our minds. "Again and again we can return to this present moment," wrote Pema Chödrön.[12]

Once we are free from our minds' ongoing chatter, the fresh breeze of the Spirit can blow into us and through us. We become wind instruments making musical harmony with one another. Being present opens an inner freedom and spaciousness. It creates a well-being that is independent of circumstances, thoughts, and even emotions. Being present allows us to access the untapped wells of joy already within us, just waiting to be opened.

The Practice of Presence

If we want to start learning to be more present in our daily lives, this has to become a disciplined practice; it doesn't just happen automatically. Trying to keep our minds in the present is a bit like trying to keep a ball at the top of a hill—it keeps slipping off, and then you have to return it there, over and over. Our automatic mode is to be in the past or the future, not in the *now*. So to break this life-long habit, we have to practice returning to the present. A regular daily practice such as Centering Prayer or meditation helps us clear the clutter and find freedom from our minds. As we do this on a daily basis, it becomes patterned into our beings. More and more, we develop the ability to hit the reset button and return to the present.

Slowing Down

I personally find it very difficult to become present in the middle of my usual busy daily activities. Sometimes my mind feels like a high-speed water skier flitting across the surface of my life. I have found that I need to allow some time to slow down enough to gradually sink into the present moment.

A helpful first step is to set aside time to intentionally shift from the usual multitasking mode, choosing instead to do one thing at a time (single-tasking) for a certain period of time. While you are doing this, try to do your activities a bit more slowly, sinking into each experience. I have found that silent retreats offer a wonderful opportunity for this kind of slowing down.

Gerald May wrote:

> What I am experiencing is the Power of the Slowing, yet I have no idea what it means. I cannot get my mind around it—and that also feels absolutely right. It mystifies me, and I am further mystified by my enjoyment of being mystified. Here is something that I am feeling so strongly, and I don't understand it at all. And I don't need to—a great relief for a psychiatrist. I have been beautifully, exquisitely mystified. . . . I don't remember ever feeling

so free, but I don't really care about that either. All I know is there's confidence in this moment, lightness inside and out. I have been slowed down. I have been slowed by a Power.[13]

Leisure Time

Leisure is also an important way to slow down and become present. Michael Fish, a Camaldolese monk, has a saying I find helpful: "Leisure is the precursor to contemplation."

Picture a garden bed full of hard, dry clods. Anyone who has worked in a garden knows it's not easy preparing sunbaked soil like this for planting. If you want to soften these flinty lumps of earth, you can't just give them a quick spray of water; that will only moisten the outside but won't penetrate the clods' hard centers. The only thing that softens soil like this is prolonged exposure to rain. After a few days of steady rain, a hoe will break the hard dirt. Now, the soft, loamy earth is ready to grow healthy plants.

The hectic pace of our everyday lives can leave us feeling arid and clenched inside. A few occasional moments of presence and stillness will not soften us at a deep level. Daily Centering Prayer, however, will soak our hearts like gentle rain, and so does leisure time—time when we choose to do nothing "productive," when we simply relax (preferably somewhere in Nature), looking, listening, and slowly settling down enough to become present. This "deep soaking" in presence allows us to return to our busy lives with a renewed ability to be mindful and aware.

The Pause

We don't always have the luxury of leisure time in the busy pace of our day-to-day lives. A practice called "the Pause"[14] allows us to interrupt the auto-pilot mode of living and return to being present, even for a few moments, before continuing with our daily activities. This is a short practice that can wake us up from the storylines that so easily ensnare us.

To do this, we stop what we are doing for a few moments, in order to become aware of where we are, how our bodies feel, and what is happening within us. We might also take a few moments to reconnect with an awareness of our breathing before continuing with our daily activities.

This brief practice can never be a substitute for the nourishing richness of more lengthy periods of leisure and stillness, but it is an important tool for helping us return to presence in the midst of our hectic lives. As Brother Lawrence said, "God will use the briefest moment."[15]

Any moment that we are present,
we are being fed.
The grace that we receive when we are present
feels like being nourished—

our soul and heart being nourished by reality.
If we are with what is happening now,
we are getting the ingredients that we need to arise,
come together, and return.
If we're not present,
no matter what experience we have,
it will never satisfy our craving inside.
What fulfils us is the quality of our openness,
receptivity and attention
in whatever experience we are having.
It doesn't come from the content of the experience.

—RUSS HUDSON[16]

INVITATION TO PRACTICE

These exercises are opportunities for you to practice presence.

Mindful Tea/Coffee Drinking

Make yourself a cup of tea or coffee, exactly the way you like it. Find somewhere to sit where you are relaxed and comfortable. Drink your tea very slowly, swallow by swallow, bringing your attention to the smell and the flavor of the tea, savoring it fully. Try not to think about the next mouthful or the time when your tea is finished or how you should drink all of your cups of tea this way. Just stay with this mouthful, and enjoy it.

Mindful Walking Exercise

Find a place where you can walk in a relaxed and unself-conscious way. Begin by standing still for a while and becoming aware of your surroundings. Take a few deep breaths. Now bring your attention to how your body feels. Move your shoulders around a bit to relax them, twist at your waist a few times, and bend forward at your hips to feel a slight stretch up the backs of your legs. Stand in a relaxed way, and when you are ready, walk forward slowly, in time with your breathing.

When you breathe in, take a slow, steady step. Bring your attention to the soles of your feet, and become aware of the contact between your foot and the ground. Bring your attention down from the level of the brain to the bottoms of your feet. When you breathe out, take another slow step, feeling the movement throughout your body as you do this. Again, become aware of the contact between your foot and the ground.

Continue walking slowly like this for at least ten minutes. When you notice your mind drifting, gently let go of the thoughts and bring your attention back to the feeling of your body as you walk.

Body Awareness Exercise[17]

First quiet yourself through bringing your awareness to different sensations in various parts of your body. Pick up even the
subtlest sensations, not just the most evident ones.

Now gently move your hands and fingers so that your
hands come to rest on your lap, palms facing upward, fingers
joined together. The movement must be very, very, slow, like
the opening of the petals of a flower. While the movement
is going on, be aware of each part of it. Once your hands are
resting on your lap, palms facing upward, become aware of
the sensations in the palms.

Then become aware of the gesture itself: this is a gesture of prayer to God that is common to most cultures and
religions. What meaning does this gesture have for you? What
are you saying to God through it? Say it without words, merely
identifying with the gesture.

Am I Breathing?

From time to time, ask yourself the question: "Am I breathing?"
This immediately puts you in touch with the sensation of your
breathing, which helps you let go of whatever your mind has
been busy with, anchoring you back in the present moment.

Ten-Minute Exercise with Your Senses

Find somewhere to sit where you are comfortable and
relaxed. In this exercise you will spend two minutes focusing

on each of your senses. It will be helpful to have a timer you can set for two-minute intervals.

Sight: Spend two minutes just looking at what is around you. If your mind wanders, gently let go of the thoughts and bring your attention back to what you are seeing. Try not to name anything or think about how beautiful or ugly it is. Just look.

Sound: Spend two minutes just listening to the sounds that are around you. Start with sounds that are nearby, and then gradually notice the sounds that are further away. If your mind wanders, gently let go of the thoughts and bring your attention back to what you are hearing. Again try not to name anything or to judge the sounds in any way. Just listen.

Touch: Spend two minutes becoming aware of what your skin is feeling. You might feel the texture of your clothes against your body, the ground under your feet, or the breeze against your skin. You could also get a sense of the air temperature and become aware of how this feels to your body. If your mind wanders, gently let go of the thoughts and bring your attention back to your sense of touch. Just feel.

Taste: Spend two minutes becoming aware of what your mouth is tasting. At first, you might think there is no taste, since you are not eating or drinking something, but after a while, you should notice a subtle flavor in your mouth. Spend time being aware of this flavor. If your mind wanders, gently let go of the thoughts and bring your attention back to awareness of the flavor in your mouth. Just taste.

Smell: Spend two minutes becoming aware of any odors your nose is sensing. If you don't notice any scents, try sniffing the grass or a nearby flower. If your mind wanders, gently let go of the thoughts and bring your attention back to awareness of your sense of smell. Just smell.

NOTES

1. Cynthia Bourgeault. *Mystical Hope: Trusting in the Mercy of God* (Lanham, MD: Cowley, 2001), p. 12.

2. Dipa Ma. "Sitting Meditations Instructions,"*Dipama* (April 5, 2022), https://dipama.com/still-guiding/.

3. Mark Williams, quoted in "What Is Mindfulness," *About Being,* https://www.ronidonnenfeld.com/what-is-mindfulness. Mindfulness-based cognitive therapy is now regarded as one of the most effective long-term strategies for dealing with issues such as depression and anxiety, and as a way of helping people who live with chronic pain.

4. Thich Nhat Hanh. *Present Moment Wonderful Moment: Mindfulness Verses for Daily Living* (Berkeley, CA: Parallax Press, 2006).

5. Ellyn Sanna. *Brother Lawrence: Christian Zen Master* (Vestal, NY: Anamchara Books, 2011), p. 41.

6. Ibid., p. 43.

7. Thomas Merton. *The Intimate Merton: His Life from His Journals* (New York: HarperCollins, 2011), August 25, 1958 entry.

8. Anthony de Mello. *Awareness: The Perils and Opportunities of Reality* (New York: Image Books, 1990), p. 90.

9. Richard Rohr "Stream of Consciousness," from his Daily Meditations (February 8, 2017), https://cac.org/daily-meditations/.

10. Cynthia Bourgeault. *Centering Prayer and Inner Awakening* (Cambridge, MA: Cowley, 2004), p. 131.

11. Sanna, p. 60.

12. Pema Chödrön. *When Things Fall Apart: Heart Advice for Difficult Times* (Boulder, CO: Shambhala, 2016), p. 105.

13. Gerald May. *The Wisdom of Wilderness: Experiencing the Healing Power of Nature* (New York: HarperCollins, 2009), p. 16.

14. "The Pause" is one of the practices described by Trish Bartley, http://trishbartley.co.uk/?q=mindfulness.

15. Sanna, p. 56.

16. Russ Hudson, from a talk in the series *The Enneagram and Grace: 9 Journeys to Divine Presence* (Louisville, CO: Sounds True, 2012).

17. Adapted from Anthony de Mello's exercise in *Sadhana: A Way to God* (New York: Image, 2011).

PART IV

Letting Go

13

Acceptance

Giving joyful thanks to the Father,
who has qualified you to participate
in the inheritance of his holy people
in the kingdom of light.

—Colossians 1:12

The Greek word translated as "inheritance" in this verse is *kléros*, which refers to your lot in life—your allotment or share. It's the same Greek word used for the gambling game the Roman soldiers played when they cast lots for Jesus' robe at the crucifixion. Unlike our usual understanding of *inheritance* in English, the Greek word involves a sense of chance, of randomness.

In *The Iliad*, Homer described this process: the people involved in a lucky draw wrote their names on a piece of broken wood or clay, put these together into a vase, which was then shaken, and the person whose lot first fell out on the ground was the one chosen. This is the same method the apostles used to choose their new twelfth member after Judas had left the scene (Acts 1:26). There is a sense of playful chance in this, of leaving it up to fate and yet trusting a deeper sense of God's will to come through the gamble.

If you link this with the shape of your life as it is right now, an enormous amount of "chance," in both nature and nurture, went into developing the "you" that you are. Your genes are a scrambled mix of possibilities out of which your unique genetic material emerged. Many of the events in your life may have seemed random and chaotic, but they nevertheless shaped you, your impression of life, and your reactive patterns. This whole ensemble of chance elements is your "inheritance," the lot apportioned to you in life. It is the reality into which you are called to participate. And yet, woven into that, for those of us on a faith journey, is the sense of God's will guiding and undergirding our lives.

Determinism, Chaos, and God's Will

Holding together these two concepts—randomness and God's will—opens up difficult questions: *Does God cause the suffering that happens in our lives? And if not, is life just one big out-of-control gamble?* Both options are frightening and leave us feeling as if we live in an unsafe universe.

Physicists grapple with questions like these. Newtonian physics was highly deterministic; scientists believed if you were given the initial conditions of any situation, and you knew the mathematical relationship between the entities involved, you could predict with certainty the future outcome at any point in time. However, quantum physics revolutionized all that, bringing in elements of uncertainty, randomness, and chaos. Einstein himself struggled with this when he was working with quantum theory, and he was so appalled by the random nature of it that he couldn't bring himself to fully agree with his own ideas. "God does not play dice with the universe," he insisted.[1]

Using a more nondual way of knowing, however, we don't need to find rational answers to these kinds of paradoxical questions. Instead, we allow them to remain open, allowing the paradoxes to draw us into a deeper mystery—the mystery where somehow God is threaded through every spontaneous event, every surprising toss of the dice. Divine creativity unfolds as reality does, not in a controlling, deterministic way, according to some Divine blueprint, but in a way that embraces and inhabits the very randomness with immediate Presence, with the assurance that no matter what emerges from this moment, the shape of the next moment will be held in the creative mercy of God. Spiritual teacher A. H. Almaas wrote:

> Maybe God is so intelligent that He [sic] can create the universe moment to moment without any blueprint! This is not to say that there is no thread running through everything that happens. The thread is nothing but exactly what is happening now, where you are in

this moment, and how this moment unfolds. As you understand what your state is right now, and follow it as it unfolds, you are following your thread.[2]

We are invited to grow into the assurance that no matter what chaos this moment gives rise to, God is able to work everything together for good, as Romans 8:28 puts it. And so we are invited to participate with what unfolds, here and now, to open our hearts and minds to the depth dimension that exists in every moment, no matter what its content may be, knowing we are unshakably held in God. Our well-being and essential identity rest in the love of God and not in the circumstances of our lives.

Richard Rohr talks about the need to fall *through* our life circumstances *into* our Real Life, the Life that is secure, unassailable, and rooted in the love and mercy of God.[3] If we learn to live in the present moment, from the deepest center that is rooted in God, we have nothing to fear from the random chaos of life. We are not involved in a terrifying game of chess between God and Satan, where we wait in terror to see who makes the best move. The human mind has conjured up frightening images of the universe, but contemplative knowing takes us into a lighter, more playful sense of life. As Thomas Merton put it:

For the world and time are the dance of the Lord in emptiness. The silence of the spheres is the music of a wedding feast. The more we persist in misunderstanding the phenomena of life, the more we analyze them out into strange finalities and complex purposes of our own, the more we involve ourselves in sadness, absurdity, and despair. But it does not matter much, because no despair of ours can alter the reality of things, or stain the joy of the cosmic dance which is always there. Indeed, we are in the midst of it, and it is in the midst of us, for it beats in our very blood, whether we want it to or not. Yet the fact remains that we are invited to forget ourselves on purpose, cast our awful solemnity to the winds and join in the general dance.[4]

But how do we shift from our fear of life's chaos into reveling in the Divine dance? How do we fall through our life circumstances into our Real Life?

Participation in the Divine Dance

When we look at the shape of our lives, we tend to reject the bits we are ashamed of, as well as the parts we think don't belong in the stories we've told ourselves about our lives. We also avoid the stuff that scares us. We project the parts of ourselves we are proud of—or at least think of as acceptable to others—and we try to plan our lives so that the good things happen more frequently.

This keeps us locked in cycles of habitual behavior. It also keeps us stuck at the superficial level of our lives' circumstances, hoping the bad stuff won't happen while trying to force the good stuff to happen. We try to load the dice, to second-guess the wheel of fortune, so that the game goes in our favor.

Ironically, the way to break out of this rut is to bring our full acceptance to our lives just as they are, allowing ourselves to experience circumstances as they unfold. James Finley described this as a process whereby God comes to us *in our lives* and *as our lives*.[5] In each unfurling moment, God gives God-self completely to us.

This means that the extent to which we can open our hearts to receive this life, as it is here and now, is the extent to which we can receive the fullness of God, in all the mystery and wonder of who God is. As soon as we second-guess life, we are resisting the flow, trying to control a dance that only makes sense when it is utterly free and unpredictable, led by God as our wild and adventurous dance partner. So the invitation is to participate with this dance by opening ourselves to each moment and accepting it. Whatever may arise outside of us and within us, we welcome each circumstance fully into our beings without trying to fix it or control it. This includes accepting the inheritance of who we each are, in the totality of our individual humanity and frailty.

Matt Licata, a psychotherapist and spiritual teacher, put it like this:

> The work, then, is not to see how quickly you can convert
> the fear to courage, the uncertainty to certainty, or the
> unknown into the known. Or to see how fast you can

cover over your vulnerability or "heal" your sensitivity, or to abandon the groundlessness for some sort of resolved state where only the feelings you like are present. For the freedom you are longing for will never be found by means of this project of conversion. Rather, this freedom—and aliveness—is already here, is uncaused, and is waiting for you in the unconditional commitment to fully participating in the truth of your experience as it is, whether it conforms to your hopes, fears, and preferences, or not. The movement of love is untamed and wildly creative—spinning out of the unknown—and is never going to conform to the way we thought it would be.[6]

We learn to trust this dance by coming to know God at a deeper level than doctrine or theory, so that we become rooted and anchored in the love of God to the point of knowing, not just with our heads but with our whole beings, that nothing can separate us from the love of God. This is a profound level of hope—not the kind of hope we call optimism, believing that things will go smoothly and according to plan, but rather an abiding hope, a hope *in* rather than a hope *that*.

Letting go of our schemes and control may sound frightening, but I have discovered it is a tremendous relief. I stop bashing my head against a wall, trying to control things that can't be controlled. Still deeper than that relief is the creative beauty of life's dance. It is as exquisite and chaotic as the unfolding process of creation itself—starting from the formless void, through the energetic chaos of the Big Bang, and blossoming into the intricate beauty and complexity of what we see in Nature.

The more I engage with this process of welcoming life as it is in this moment, the more I sense a deep trust forming in me. Profound beauty and freedom are possible, at an experiential level, precisely because I am not in control.

> *If God said,*
> *"Rumi pay homage to everything*
> *that has helped you enter my arms,"*
> *there would not be one experience of my life,*
> *not one thought, not one feeling, nor any act,*
> *I would not bow to.*
>
> —RUMI[7]

INVITATION TO REFLECT

Spend a while sitting still and focusing gently on your breathing, allowing yourself to become quiet inside.

Then bring to mind any recent areas of your life you find difficult to accept—circumstances that have felt raw, contradictory, or painful in some way. Hold these gently in your awareness for a while.

Then, as you continue to hold these areas in your awareness, listen to the Alanis Morissette song "Thank U." (You can listen to the song at https://www.youtube.com/watch?v=OOgpT5rEKIU.)

Are you able to express gratitude in a similar way for the difficult areas of your own life? Express your response to God in some way.

Now allow yourself to become quiet again, remaining still, open, and receptive to God for a few minutes.

NOTES

1. Albert Einstein. Letter to Paul Epstein, written in 1945, quoted in "God 'does not play dice with the universe,' Einstein writes in letter up for auction," *Fox News* (June 12, 2019), https://www.foxnews.com/science/einstein-letter-auction.

2. A. H. Almaas. *Facets of Unity: The Enneagram of Holy Ideas* (Boulder, CO: Shambhala,), p. 121.

3. Richard Rohr. *Falling Upward: A Spirituality for the Two Halves of Life* (New York: Wiley, 2011), p. 19.

4. Thomas Merton. *New Seeds of Contemplation* (New York: New Directions, 2007), p. 297.

5. James Finley. "Dualistic and Nondual Thinking," *Daily Meditations* (February 3, 2017), https://cac.org/daily-meditations/.

6. Matt Licata, from his blog *A Loving Healing Space*, May 19, 2016.

7. Jelal al-Din Rumi. *Love Poems from God: Twelve Sacred Voices from the East and West*, Daniel Ladinsky, trans. (New York: Penguin Compass), p. 68.

14

Surrender

How do we find
what is supposedly already there?
How do we awaken
our deepest and most profound selves?
By praying and meditating?
By more silence, solitude, and sacraments?
Yes to all, but the most important way
is to live and fully accept our reality.
This solution sounds so simple and innocuous
that most of us fabricate
all kinds of religious trappings
to avoid taking up our own inglorious,
mundane, and ever-present cross.

—Richard Rohr[1]

Somehow many of us have developed a mindset that life *should* go well, that if we plan correctly and live good lives things should run smoothly and pan out more or less in the way we want. From childhood, we have the happily-ever-after myth drummed into us, and our religious training has reinforced this with the belief that if we do good, God will bless us; if we discover the will of God and live obediently, then everything will fall into place like a well-oiled machine.

Despite all the evidence to the contrary from our lived experiences, we still hold on to these fictitious expectations. So when something goes awry, we ask ourselves questions like:

> *Where did I go wrong?*
> *What did I do to anger God?*
> *When did I step outside of God's will?*
> *Why me?*

Our expectations of life are rather childlike and primitive. A far more realistic perspective is expressed with the statement "Shit happens." Life does not go smoothly. No matter how good we are, or how carefully we plan, trying to foresee all the possible outcomes, life has a way of throwing us surprises. That's just the way life is.

This acknowledgment of life's reality calls us to a new response. Pain, suffering, frustration, and disappointment are givens (shit is bound to happen), and that awareness now becomes the backdrop of our perceptions. That's how it is, so why keep fighting it?

This is sometimes called the "suchness of life." As Buddhist teacher Stephen Levine put it, "God is not someone or something separate but is the suchness in each moment, the underlying reality."[2]

Letting Go

When we encounter surprises and unexpected turns in our lives, we have two choices: resist what is happening, fighting against it—or yield to what is, letting go of our expectations, frustrations, and perceived "rights" and going with the flow. Cynthia Bourgeault refers to this as *surrender*, and she pointed out that "the word 'surrender' itself means to 'hand oneself over' or 'entrust oneself.'" She went on to say that surrender "is not about outer capitulation but about inner opening."[3]

Life with all its unpredictability is a continual open invitation to surrender. This is a more adventurous way of living, because it is more open-ended, loaded with surprises around the next corner. On the other hand, as the Buddha pointed out, when we resist the suchness of life, we cause ourselves suffering.

We have all sorts of lists of conditions for our happiness. We will one day be happy, we tell ourselves, if we look like this, if we own that car or house, if we have a better job. Or we will be happy if our partners learn to be the way we want them to be, if our neighbors stop doing that irritating thing, or if we attain spiritual perfection. But we are invited to let go of our lists of requirements and our resistance to what is actually happening—and instead welcome everything that cannot be changed.

Life gives us endless opportunities to practice letting go, over and over. Each letting go is a gift to us, because it further dismantles our over-involved egos that want so much to be in control. Life becomes a wonderful range of opportunities for spiritual growth, for opening more to the mysterious ways of God, which are always more spacious and wise than we can imagine or predict.

This attitude of surrender creates freedom. We are in a very constricted space when we believe our happiness and sense of "okay-ness" depend on things working out as we want them to. This belief allows little room for alternatives. As a result, we become imprisoned by our expectations. Yielding to life's suchness, on the other hand, allows us to discover an enormous space outside our narrow expectations and plans. As we let go of our knee-jerk responses of anger, frustration, and disappointment, we experience the expansiveness and spaciousness of God and of life. We find peace in the midst of chaos.

The inner movement in this process is one from the smallness of our ego-driven, self-absorbed lives into the largeness of life in God. It's not an easy movement to make; it asks that we let go of our pride and our sense of our own rights. Each time we do this, however, we discover more of our true selves, which tend to be hidden and overruled by the ego-self. Every letting go is an opportunity for the real self to emerge. Everything life brings us is an opportunity for growth and has the power to transform us—*especially* when we are out of control!

This attitude of welcoming and surrender does not mean we have a passive indifference to life. Instead, our approach to life is encapsulated in the Serenity Prayer:

> God, grant me the courage to change the things I
> can change.
> Grant me the serenity to accept the things I can-
> not change.
> Grant me the wisdom to know the difference.

Of course, no one can let go of the ego's claims all at once. We don't always even know what we are holding on to; we have lots of blind spots. The reality of life as it is, however, is our ongoing spiritual discipline. Moment by moment, we are invited to surrender to whatever life brings to us.

> *To some people,*
> *surrender may have negative connotations,*
> *implying defeat, giving up,*
> *failing to rise to the challenges of life,*
> *becoming lethargic, and so on.*
> *True surrender, however,*
> *is something entirely different.*
> *It does not mean to passively put up*

with whatever situation you find yourself in
and to do nothing about it.
Nor does it mean to cease making plans
or initiating positive action.
Surrender is the simple but profound wisdom
of yielding to rather than opposing the flow of life.

—ECKHART TOLLE[4]

INVITATION TO PRACTICE

Gently focus on your breathing for a while, and allow yourself to become still.

Now gather together in your mind a sense of your life as it is right now. Hold the whole of it open to God, and slowly pray the Welcoming Prayer:

Welcome, welcome, welcome.
I welcome everything that comes to me in this moment
because I know it is for my healing.
I welcome all thoughts, feelings, emotions,
persons, situations and conditions.
I let go of my desire for security.
I let go of my desire for approval.
I let go of my desire for control.
I let go of my desire to change any situation,

condition, person, or myself.

I open to the love and presence of God

and the healing action and grace within.[5]

NOTES

1. Richard Rohr. "Center and Circumference," from his Daily Meditations (April 30, 2013), https://cac.org/daily-meditations/.

2. Stephen Levine. *Healing into Life and Death* (New York: Anchor, 1987), p. 107.

3. Cynthia Bourgeault. *The Wisdom Way of Knowing: Reclaiming an Ancient Tradition to Awaken the Heart* (San Francisco, CA: Jossey-Bass,), p. 72.

4. Eckhart Tolle. *The Power of Now: A Guide to Spiritual Enlightenment* (Novato, CA: New World Library, 2010), p. 205.

5. Taken from http://contemplativeoutreach.org.uk/leaflets/WelcomePrayer.pdf.

15

Resignation

God has not created us for self-dominion,
but as instruments of his wonder

—JAKOB BÖHME[1]

The German mystic Jacob Boehme focused much of his writing on a practice he called "resignation." While we may connect this word with either quitting a job or accepting something we don't like, the original meaning had to do with giving up something, with surrendering or relinquishing a claim or right. Boehme used the word to refer to the total surrendering of our wills to God's will, echoing the prayer of Jesus in the garden of Gethsemane: "Not my will, but yours be done" (Luke 22:42).

I used to think of "doing the will of God" as donning a heavy, scratchy cloak of moralistic rules and heavy expectations that felt life-draining and bleak. To my delight, however, I have discovered that being in a state of complete surrender to the Divine Will is an utterly energized state of being from which life spontaneously springs. Cynthia Bourgeault described this resignation of the ego's will as "an immediate and direct opening, at an energetic level, to the Source of all being."[2]

Letting Go of "My Will"

Our modern-day Western minds go: "What? What? Being made to do what I don't want to do—how can that be energizing?" But we need to understand what we mean by "will." The self-constructed "me" we try so hard to defend, protect, and keep comfortable and happy is the preoccupation of the calculating mind, keeping us locked in cycles of reactivity and unhappiness because we think this "me" is all there is. This is the "me" that wants to do what it wants to do.

And so releasing our grip on our own wills and instead, surrendering—or resigning—to the Divine Will, sets us free to enter the vast, mysterious, and life-giving realm of God, which our calculating minds cannot grasp. I have been using as a mantra this wonderful line from Boehme: "The soul must remain in resigned humility just as the fountain depends on its source."[3]

This is the process of dying to self: a complete resignation (a letting go, a surrender) of our clutching, grasping, self-centered wills. As we release our claims to control and success, we enter a vast, open place that at first feels like nothing—but is full of the something of

God. In the total release of our grip on our small, constricted wills, we are freed to experience the spaciousness of God. The fountain of Divine life and love bursts forth from this space into our lives.

Real life and love can only be found in this state of complete resignation to the Divine Will. As Boehme wrote, "No work outside of God's will can reach God's kingdom. It is all only a useless carving in the great laboriousness of man [sic]."[4]

As I worked with this notion of resignation, I wrote these notes in my journal:

> I have been realizing that all my attempts to live this life, to make it work in any way, are faulty and doomed to failure, because they all have me at the center of the picture. This is not a fault as much as a product of my human way of being in the world. Only by resigning from this role as CEO of Sharon's life, resigning to God's ways, is there any hope. And God's ways can only arise from the Quiet Center when I have let go of my own efforts and self-referential ways.

Centering Prayer, which we looked at in chapter 10, is a practice that helps us develop our ability to release our will. In her book on this method of quiet prayer, Cynthia Bourgeault wrote:

> Letting go of a thought is a small but powerful symbol of our willingness in a larger sense to let go of our own stuff

and return to that open attending upon God. I sometimes call Centering Prayer "boot camp in Gethsemane," for it practices over and over, thought by thought, the basic gesture of Jesus' night of struggle in the garden: "Not my will be done, Oh Lord, but thine." . . .

Dying to self means being willing to let go of what I want (or think I want) in order to create space for God to direct, lead, and guide me into a truer way of being. . . . You do not die on a cross in order to "set up" the resurrection; you die on a cross because the willingness to give it all away is itself the original and ultimate creative act from which all being flows.[5]

Another way in which we can practice the resignation of our wills is to welcome whatever arises. This needs to happen at two levels, the outer and the inner.

On the outer level, resignation means giving up our efforts to control our circumstances. We resign from our position as the managing director of the world around us. Instead, we choose to "go with the flow" of life, trusting God in whatever circumstances arise. This does not mean we roll over and play dead, nor does it mean we become a doormat. We will still set healthy boundaries, but now we determine those boundaries from an inner stance of openness and receptivity. From this open place, we make clearer, wiser decisions about how to respond, instead of our usual knee-jerk way of reacting to circumstances. This wisdom comes from the contemplative place of quietness and surrender.

Meanwhile, on an inner level, resignation means welcoming whatever arises within us, no matter how disturbing or dark it feels. We surrender all our usual strategies for resistance or avoidance. So, for example, if we are feeling sad, we let that wave of sadness hit us fully in the chest. We consciously feel how it affects our body and our breathing. As much as possible, we let go of any story that is attached to the sadness, and we simply *feel* it, physically.

"You will come into the Ground out of which all things proceed," wrote Boehme.[6] This is the creative power of surrender. Every time we let go of our own wills, our clinging, grasping attempts at controlling or resisting the moment, we echo the words of Jesus, "Not my will but yours be done" (Luke 22:42), as well as the words of Mary, "May it be with me as you have said" (Luke 1:38). In doing this, we allow the life of Christ to be birthed within us. From this open place of resignation, the flourishing of God emerges, out into the world.

When you remain silent
from the thinking and willing of self,
the Eternal hearing and seeing and speaking
will be revealed in you,
and God will see and hear through you.

—Jakob Böhme[7]

INVITATION TO REFLECT

Spend a while sitting still and focusing gently on your breathing, allowing yourself to become quiet inside.

Now bring to mind a recent memory of a time when you felt a disturbing emotion. As you replay the events in your mind, try to feel your emotional response again.

Take a while to become aware of how this emotion feels in your body. Where do you feel it most vividly? What physical sensations do you experience? Let go of the story in your mind—the narrative that went along with these feelings—and stay with these sensations for a while. While you would normally resist these emotions or distract yourself so you don't have to feel them, now respond instead with an open and receptive attitude.

Mentally repeat a phrase such as "Not my will but yours be done," "May it be with me as you have said," or the Welcoming Prayer (given at the end of the last chapter). As you do this, what is your experience?

Finally, allow yourself to become quiet again, remaining still, open, and receptive to God for a few more minutes.

NOTES

1. Jakob Böhme. (This is the German spelling of his name.) *The Way to Christ* (Mahwah, NJ: Paulist Press, 1978), p. 122.

2. Cynthia Bourgeault. "Boehme for Beginners," *Gnosis Magazine* (Fall 1997), pp. 29–35.

3. Böhme, p. 121.

4. Ibid., p. 123.

5. Cynthia Bourgeault. *Centering Prayer and Inner Awakening* (Cambridge, MA: Cowley, 2004), p. 49.

6. Böhme, p. 179.

7. Ibid., p. 171.

16

Kenosis

Your attitude
should be the same as that of Christ Jesus:
Who, being in very nature God,
did not consider equality with God
something to be used to his own advantage;
rather, he made himself nothing . . . [and] he humbled himself
by becoming obedient to death—even death on a cross!

–PHILIPPIANS 2:5-8

In the above passage, the original phrase translated as "he made himself nothing" used a Greek verb: *kenosein*, meaning "kenosis"—to empty oneself. These verses indicate that Paul recognized that kenosis was a practice, not just an attribute belonging exclusively to Jesus. As Cynthia Bourgeault wrote:

As Paul so profoundly realizes, self-emptying is the touchstone, the core reality underlying every moment of Jesus' human journey. . . . The full realization of his divine selfhood comes not through clinging to his divine status, but through a voluntary divestment of it.[1]

We humans, especially those of us in the West, tend to have the opposite mindset. We perceive life through the lens of a scarcity mentality, believing there is not enough of everything (money, time, achievements, whatever). At the same time, we fear that at any moment what we value will be taken from us. As we look at our lives through this lens, we resist and constrict whenever anything happens that doesn't align with our idea of how life should be. As we noted earlier, this resistance is what causes us to suffer.

We are spiritually blind, lacking a sense of the generosity and abundance of God threaded through our everyday life. We don't recognize the Divine beauty and bounty as God gives abundant life to us in every moment. Because of this, we try to surround ourselves with what we think is abundance, hoarding money and possessions, taking out insurance policies, building walls and burglar guards, and generally trying to enclose ourselves within a protective boundary of comfort and security. All this endless effort comes from our fundamental belief that we have to ensure our own well-being.

Time and time again, though, Jesus taught about the importance of giving and letting go. He often used stories to convey his message, such as this parable of the wealthy landowner:

The ground of a certain rich man yielded an abundant harvest. He thought to himself, "What shall I do? I have no place to store my crops." Then he said, "This is what I'll do. I will tear down my barns and build bigger ones, and there I will store my surplus grain. And I'll say to myself, 'You have plenty of grain laid up for many years. Take life easy; eat, drink and be merry.'" But God said to him, "You fool! This very night your life will be demanded from you. Then who will get what you have prepared for yourself?' "This is how it will be with who-ever stores up things for themselves but is not rich toward God. (Luke 12:16–21)

Just as we so often do, the rich man was looking at life through the lens of scarcity. Despite the abundance of his harvest, he feared that one day he still might not have enough. Thinking to ensure his own wealth by containing it and holding it, he in fact restricted his life. He hoarded when he might have shared with others in the true spirit of abundance.

Jesus was not saying that because the man built barns, God would punish him with death. The parables of Jesus are rich with metaphor and meaning, but they are not meant to be taken literally. Perhaps, however, the constriction of the man's outer life and inner being led to a physical constriction, one that killed him. According to the Mayo Clinic, negative thoughts create stress reactions in our bodies—and because these reactions increase the likelihood of heart disease and stroke, with time, negative thinking might literally kill someone.[2]

Like the rich man, we too perceive reality as being withholding, rather than threaded through with the abundance and generosity of God. As we cling and hoard, we become even less capable of seeing the already-given abundance of life. By building barns and stockpiling our resources, we miss out on the fullness of living in the present and receiving what is right in front of us (thereby leading to our metaphorical deaths).

The more we resist what we do not want, while clinging to what we *do* want, the more we reinforce our underlying belief that life is threatening and that God is withholding. This causes a blockage of the free flow of life through us to others, and so we become constricted, narrowed, like a blood vessel lined with plaque that restricts the flow of life-blood through the body.

Jesus is our model for a new way of responding to life. With him, we learn to pray, "Not my will but yours be done," and, "May *your* kingdom come, may *your* will be done." As we empty ourselves of our will, we open channels for God's love and abundance to flow through us—and we change our habitual perceptions of life and God.

Biological Perspectives

Magnetic resonance imaging (MRI) shows that our habitual responses to life create distinct brain patterns.[3] The limbic system, containing the amygdala, is the most primitive part of the human brain; it governs our "fight or flight" responses and is associated with anxiety and fear. If we respond to a stimulus with initial negativity or inner constriction, the stimulus will be processed through the amygdala. The more we respond with this part of our brain, the more we entrench our neural conditioning, which reinforces our emotional patterns of fear and anxiety.

If we respond with relaxation, however, with the open-handed stance of kenosis, MRIs indicate that the stimulus is processed through the more advanced part of the human forebrain, the pre-frontal cortex, which is associated with higher-order brain functions such as emotional intelligence, compassion and the ability to self-regulate.[4] Responding with this prefrontal part of the brain allows us to access emotional intelligence, generosity, creativity, and compassion.

A team of researchers at Harvard found that mindfulness meditation actually decreases the brain-cell volume in the more primitive and fearful amygdala—and these changes matched the participants' self-reports of improved stress levels.[5] Meanwhile, other research indicates that when we practice Centering Prayer or some other form of meditation, we create and reinforce neural connections within the more compassionate, intuitive prefrontal part of our brains.[6] The same study found that mindfulness meditation decreases activity in the brain network responsible for mind-wandering (what meditation teachers often call the "monkey mind") and self-referential ("me-centered") thoughts. Meditation nurtures and enhances the prefrontal areas of our brains, giving us greater access to intelligence and creative abilities.

"Don't Be Afraid"

While the fear of physical danger is a healthy reaction to a specific and actual threat, anxiety is a habitual response that focuses on what *might* happen in the future. Anxiety clings to negative, fearful thoughts, repeating them over and over while preventing us from being present to the right-now moment. Worrying somehow gives us the illusion we can control the future, as we saw in the parable about the rich man. In reality, however, anxiety is not only nonproductive but physically and emotionally destructive.

Fear triggers our bodies to prepare for actual danger. Respiration and heart rate accelerate, to bring more energy to our muscles, and our muscles tighten, getting ready to either fight or run away. Blood flow decreases to our brains' frontal lobes, which are responsible for logical thinking and planning, and is redirected to the more instinctive parts of our brains, including the amygdala. Blood flow to our stomachs and intestines is also diminished; if we're running for our lives, our bodies don't want to waste energy digesting our breakfasts. All these responses are healthy and useful when we're encountering an actual danger—but unfortunately, our bodies can't tell the difference between fear and anxiety. When we worry, we put ourselves in a constant state of physiological fear reaction. The same reactions that are helpful when our bodies are preparing to deal with a short-lived crisis become destructive when habitual worry makes those reactions constant. Heart disease, gastrointestinal problems, high blood pressure, and emotional disorders are just some of the effects of chronic anxiety.

In the kenosis of Centering Prayer, however, we let go of anxiety's repetitive and destructive thoughts. Spiritual practices and disciplines are not just there to test our obedience or austerity. They are guidelines for living a healthy, connected, and generous life, physically, emotionally, and spiritually. They create new space within our bodies and minds for well-being, creativity, and compassion.

Perhaps this is why the most frequent command in the Bible is "Fear not." Anxiety interrupts our connection with God. It blocks our perception of Divine love, as Jesus affirmed.

> Are not five sparrows sold for two pennies? Yet not one of them is forgotten by God. Indeed, the very hairs of your head are all numbered. Don't be afraid; you are worth more than many sparrows. (Luke 12:6–7)

Inner constriction and clinging create anxiety, our sense of scarcity and threat. When we consciously choose to relax our egos' grip on our lives, when instead we practice openness and generosity, we refocus our perceptions. Now, we can begin to recognize the abundance of God and of life; we perceive the tenderness of God's care for even the sparrows. As we practice this letting-go in daily prayer, our brain patterns change. We replace habitual anxiety with an ongoing attitude of kenosis, as Jesus modeled for us. This is the path to true inner freedom and joy.

> When the "fight or flight" alarm bells
> are going off in your head
> and everything inside
> you wants to brace and defend itself,
> the infallible way to extricate yourself . . .
> is simply to freely release
> whatever you are holding onto. . . .
> The method of full, voluntary self-donation
> reconnects you instantly to the wellspring;
> in fact, it is the wellspring.
>
> —CYNTHIA BOURGEAULT[7]

INVITATION TO REFLECT

Spend a while sitting still and focusing gently on your breathing, allowing yourself to become quiet inside.

Now bring to mind any areas of your life where you are aware of a habitual reaction of hoarding or clinging. What emotions do you experience when you are in the grip of this constricted reaction?

Now, clench your fists to demonstrate a hoarding, constricted inner state—and then release your fists and open your arms out to express a willingness to let go. Try this gesture while reflecting on your own areas of constriction. What do you experience as you shift from the gesture of clinging to letting go?

Take some time to write about your reflections in your journal. Then allow yourself to become quiet again, remaining still, open, and receptive to God for a few minutes.

NOTES

1. Cynthia Bourgeault. *The Meaning of Mary Magdalene: Discovering the Woman at the Heart of Christianity* (Boulder, CO: Shambhala, 2010), p. 103.

2. Mayo Clinic staff. "Positive Thinking," *Healthy Lifestyle: Stress Management,* https://www.mayoclinic.org/.

3. See, for example: https://blogs.scientificamerican.com/guest-blog/what-does-mindfulness-meditation-do-to-your-brain/

4. For more on this, see Dan Siegel's *The Developing Mind: How Relationships and the Brain Interact to Shape Who We Are* (NY: Guilford Press, 2020).

5. Sue McGreevey. "Eight Weeks to a Better Brain" *The Harvard Gazette* (January 21, 2011), http://news.harvard.edu/gazette/.

6. Kaitlin McLean. "The Healing Art of Meditation," *Yale Scientific* (May 10, 2012), http://www.yalescientific.org/.

7. Cynthia Bourgeault. *Centering Prayer and Inner Awakening* (Cambridge, MA: Cowley, 2004), p. 87.

PART V

The Invitation to Know Ourselves Deeply

17

Self-Awareness

He also told them this parable:
"Can the blind lead the blind?
Will they not both fall into a pit?
. . . Why do you look at the speck of sawdust
in your brother's eye
and pay no attention to the plank in your own eye?
How can you say to your brother,
'Brother, let me take the speck out of your eye,'
when you yourself fail to see the plank in your own eye?
You hypocrite, first take the plank out of your eye,
and then you will see clearly
to remove the speck from your brother's eye."

—LUKE 6:39-42

When I read these verses, I imagine someone with a huge log sticking out of their eye trying to help somebody who has a tiny speck in their eye. But what is so wrong with trying to help others to change and grow? Well, the problem with having huge logs in our eyes is that we have become used to them. Often, we are completely blinded by them, so blind, in fact, that we don't even perceive that the logs are there.

Before anything else, we need to see that we can't see! We must recognize that our vantage points are compromised by the mere fact that we are human and we experience life from the subjectivity of our individual bodies. As a result, we look out at life from our own sets of needs, experiences, and assumptions, and then we generalize these.

In addition to this, we want to control what happens around us, to keep our lives safe and predictable, and so we try to change other people to fit how we think reality should be.

The Illusion of Asymmetric Insight

The illusion of asymmetric insight is "a cognitive bias whereby people perceive their knowledge of others to surpass other people's knowledge of them."[1] Studies have found that people tend to believe they know themselves better than their peers know themselves. In addition to this, people believe their social group knows and understands other social groups better than other social groups know them.

Science journalist David McRaney wrote:

You feel like the other person must have been tainted in some way, otherwise they would see the world the way you do—the right way. The illusion of asymmetrical insight clouds your ability to see the people you disagree with as nuanced and complex. You tend to see your self and the groups you belong to in shades of grey, but others and their groups as solid and defined primary colors lacking nuance or complexity. . . . Remember, you are not so smart, and what seems like an insight is often an illusion.[2]

This is the problem with trying to clean the speck out of somebody else's eye. We assume what we can see is the problem, but in reality, the other person has layers of complexity hidden beneath the surface, an entire inner world we know nothing about. It's sheer arrogance to assume we can go around dusting somebody else's furniture when we don't know anything about the earth tremors that rock their world.

Our vantage point is limited, and our assumptions about ourselves and others are faulty and unbalanced (asymmetrical). Realizing that is the first step toward self-awareness.

Removing the Support Beams

When Jesus talked about the log in someone's eye, he used a Greek word, *dokos*, that meant "support beam or rafter." Jesus could have said, "First remove the stick from your own eye," and we would have gotten his message, but as a carpenter, Jesus would have known about the different kinds of logs and beams used for various purposes. By referring to a support beam, a massive, sturdy piece of wood, he made his analogy all the more extreme.

What's more, he added another layer of meaning. You can't go around removing support beams from a building, because they are load-bearing and necessary for keeping the whole structure in place. But in this case, the building—the structure we have built, which is our self-focused ego—needs to come down. This structure, which houses our own self-importance, skews our perceptions. We need to remove the supporting beams, so that the entire edifice collapses.

The self-constructed identity is often described as the *false self*. Unless the false self is dismantled, we will remain blinded by the support beams and rafters of our self-interest. The collapse of the false identity is what Jesus was talking about when he said, "Unless a grain of wheat falls into the earth and dies, it remains just a grain of wheat; but if it dies, it bears much fruit" (John 12:24).

What Blinds Us?

Prejudice

I grew up as a typical white kid under South African apartheid. I thought the segregation of our society was normal, that it was "just the way things were." This mindset was reinforced by fears of the unknown other, and of course, by attachment to our known way of life, our comforts and power position. It didn't occur to me that white prejudice and assumptions were blinding me.

Then, in my seventh year of school, my parents sent me to the Mmabatho multiracial school, where I was the only white girl in the class. Now, I learned side by side with children from different races and language groups, and in this context, I first heard the word "apartheid." When my Malawian history teacher asked the black children in the class to share their experiences of apartheid, I was shocked to realize this was a deeply hurtful, damaging system I had accepted blindly.

A massive area of my perception of South Africa was faulty, obscured by the log of prejudice. When that log was finally removed, my vision expanded to see the humanity and suffering of everybody in our troubled society, particularly those who were marginalized and disenfranchised by the unjust system.

This is an ongoing challenge. I continue to realize new ways in which I am blind to the reality of my white privilege and the preferential treatment it still buys me, both in South African society and globally. Unfortunately, I am not alone. Racism (as well as all other forms of prejudice, including ageism, sexism, and heterosexism) completely compromises our ability to see reality as it is.

Selective Receptivity

One of the habits of the calculating mind, which is continually building and reinforcing our self-constructed self, is to evaluate everything we experience from our egocentric position. We create categories, dividing good from bad, comfortable from uncomfortable, beneficial from threatening, and so on, judging each circumstance depending on how it relates to our own self-interests. This dualistic thinking prevents us from seeing anything that doesn't fit into our categories. As Anthony de Mello wrote:

> You falsely think that your fears protect you, your beliefs have made you what you are, and your attachments make your life exciting and secure. You fail to see that they are actually a screen between you and life's symphony. . . . You see persons and things not as they are, but as you are. If you wish to see them as they are, you must attend to your attachments and the fears that your attachments generate, because these decide what you will notice and what you block out.[3]

When we continually divide each moment into what is good or bad, what we agree with or disagree with, we fail to perceive anything not in line with our egocentric agendas. We reject anything that contradicts what we already believe about reality. Consequently, our distorted perceptions of reality are even further distorted by the judgments we make using those distorted perspectives. It's a self-reinforcing loop that eventually makes us functionally blind to huge sectors of life's reality. This distortion of our perceptions leads to all kinds of hatefulness, oppression, greed, and destruction, all to maintain our interests in the world as we perceive it.

But as we do begin to recognize our minds' habits of judgment and selective seeing, we will discover more and more of the freedom that is possible.

The Dismantling Process

"If your spirit becomes unclogged and your senses open," wrote Anthony de Mello, "you will begin to perceive things as they really are and to interact with reality. . . . Then you will understand what God is, for you will at last know what love is."[4]

Here again, we must participate in the dance of grace and conscious choice. Removing support beams from our vision is not an easy task—but through the grace of God, using the "suchness" of our individual lives, we gradually dismantle the self-constructed false self, clearing our vision of the debris that kept us clogged and blind. If we allow them, the failures and humiliations that come our way will reveal the extent to which we are invested in protecting and defending the structure of our selves. These experiences, which we usually consider negative, hold up a mirror to us, showing us our hidden areas of self-centeredness and control. Rather than fighting or resisting these painful moments, we can welcome them (as we discussed in chapter 14). All of life, as it comes to us moment by moment, holds the possibility of healing and wholeness. We can choose to participate in the process—or we can resist it, clinging to our old self-centered structures.

Self-Knowledge

Theresa of Avila said, "For the most part, all the trials and disturbances come from our not understanding ourselves."[5] The cofounders of the Enneagram Institute explain why self-knowledge is so important: "Once we understand the nature of our personality's mechanisms, we begin to have a choice about identifying with them or not." But as with the logs in our eyes, we must first realize what these mechanisms are, since "If we are not aware of them, clearly no choice is possible."[6]

Self-assessments such as the Enneagram and the Myers-Briggs Type Indicator are useful tools to help us recognize our internal architecture. Journaling can also help; it gets our invisible thoughts out on paper where we can see them. We can also stand back from our thought processes and act as a witness to what is happening in our minds. Michael Singer suggests an exercise where we imagine our mind to be a roommate, and we notice how chatty and interruptive this roommate is.[7] As soon as we observe our mental chatter, we loosen its hold on us, and that in turn frees us to stop identifying with the false self.

This is not a fast or easy process. The recognition of the false self requires the excavation of layers upon layers of stuff that has accumulated over the years. Disassembling the enormous, elaborate structures we think of as ourselves is painstaking work. As we become more and more honest with ourselves, though, we more easily recognize the extent of our self-absorption and our destructive patterns.

At this point, we are often tempted to be harsh or judgmental with ourselves, but that can hinder rather than help the dismantling process. Instead of opening ourselves, we retract, focusing only on the horror of our own selves. In the process, we become blind to reality in a new way. As Richard Rohr wrote, "we have to observe, but also not let the observer become the accusing tyrant."[8] Instead, we face these dark, painful places in ourselves with kindness and compassion. We allow ourselves to fall into the hands of the gracious, loving God.

Trying to excise our misperceptions through sheer willpower is seldom helpful either. We don't have to change ourselves by rejecting and cutting out parts of ourselves; we just have to become aware of what is there. Then, as soon as we recognize a pattern, we are already interrupting the pattern's autopilot. This allows us to gradually disidentify with our self-constructed selves, which has the natural consequence of freeing us to see with greater clarity.

Scripture tells us: "The Eternal God is your dwelling place, and underneath are the everlasting arms" (Deuteronomy 33:27). The Hebrew word for everlasting, *olam*, means "vanishing point," and it speaks to both the long ages past as well as the endless ages to come—in other words, infinity. When we let our cramped, self-constructed structures collapse, we move into the infinite spaciousness of God's dwelling place.

This can feel like a leap into nothingness. We let go of the known, the predictable, and all our ego-defending constructs. It is a terrifying proposition for the self that tries to cling to life-as-it-is. And yet, as we feel ourselves fall, we drop into the vast spaciousness of the infinite arms that undergird everything.

> *We must somehow strip ourselves*
> *of our greatest illusions about ourselves, . . .*
> *descend into the depths of our being*
> *until we come to the basic reality that is in us,*
> *and learn to see that we are loveable after all,*
> *in spite of everything!*

—THOMAS MERTON[9]

INVITATION TO PRACTICE

Here are a few exercises you might find useful in the work of self awareness.

Recognize the Mind's Habits

During the next few days, try to be aware of your typical reactions or habitual thought processes.

Label whatever thought process you notice; for example, "judging", "craving," "pleased with myself," "resentful." Have a sense of humor and don't beat yourself up over anything that arises. It may be helpful to jot down a list in your journal.

After you have recognized and named a thought process, allow yourself to gently let it go. Acknowledge to yourself that it is simply an aspect of a conditioned response. It is not YOU.

If something particularly painful or difficult comes up and is too persistent to simply let go, picture holding this part of yourself with gentle compassion. Allow yourself to sense God's tender embrace.

Who Am I?

Self-inquiry is an exercise in asking ourselves the question "Who am I?" at deeper and deeper levels. Whenever you think you have arrived at an answer, the challenge is to let this go. Each "answer" is simply another layer of identification with some thought or belief.

When your mind interrupts with an objection or an argument, acknowledge that this is exactly the kind of thing the mind does when it is being questioned. Then let go of the thought and return again to holding the question open: Who am I?

NOTES

1. https://en.wikipedia.org/wiki/Illusion_of_asymmetric_insight.

2. David McRaney. "The Illusion of Asymmetric Insight," *You Are Not So Smart* (August 21, 2011), https://youarenotsosmart.com/.

3. Anthony de Mello. *The Way to Love: Meditations for Life* (New York: Crown, 2011), p. 34.

4. Ibid.

5. Theresa of Avila. *The Interior Castle,* Kieran Kavanaugh and Otilio Rodriguez, trans. (Washington, DC: ICS, 2020), p. 86.

6. Don Riso and Russ Hudson. *The Wisdom of the Enneagram: The Complete Guide to Psychological and Spiritual Growth for the Nine Personality Types* (New York: Bantam, 1999), p. 38.

7. Michael A. Singer. *The Untethered Soul Guided Journal: Practices to Journey Beyond Yourself* (Oakland, CA: New Harbinger, 2020), pp. 36–40.

8. Richard Rohr. *Everything Belongs: The Gift of Contemplative Prayer* (Chestnut Ridge, NY: Crossroad, 2003), pp. 104–105.

9. Thomas Merton. *No Man Is an Island* (New York: Harcourt, Brace, 2002), p. 213.

18

Shadow

The important thing
is to learn from your shadow side.
Some call this pattern
the discovery of the "golden shadow"
because it carries so much enlightenment for the soul. . . .
As Carl Jung put it so well,
"Where you stumble and fall,
there you find pure gold."

—RICHARD ROHR[1]

One of the things we long for most in life is freedom—but like all spiritual growth, freedom requires a difficult journey through the dark valley of the shadow of death. We have to prayerfully ask the crucial question: *What is tethering me?* We need the wisdom and guidance of the Spirit of Truth to shine light into our dark places, because this is where the answer lies. Spiritual and emotional freedom require an honest recognition and integration of our shadow areas.

To understand the shadow, we first need to look at what is sometimes called the "descriptive self." This is the image of ourselves we want people to see; it depends on external descriptions: how good we look, what we possess, how we perform, how moral we are. Other terms for the same concept are "persona" or "false self."

Within each of us there is also a "true self," the self that is "hidden with Christ in God," as Paul put it (Colossians 3:3). This true self is always in union with God, connected to the vine, as Christ's analogy in John 15 describes it. The spiritual journey gradually takes us to the place where we let go of the false self and become more aware of the true self, living from the stability and spaciousness of union with God.

However, the layers of our descriptive selves are well-developed and well-defended. Often, we are not even aware of our true self, and so we seldom experience its robust spaciousness. The descriptive sense of ourselves has been reinforced throughout our entire lifetimes, and now we are so strongly identified with it that we may not realize it isn't real.

To keep this descriptive self in place, we hide the areas in ourselves that contradict the images we like to show the world. These hidden and unacknowledged parts are what Carl Jung referred to as the shadow, an area in the unconscious mind that contains repressed weaknesses, shortcomings, and instincts. "Everyone carries a shadow," Jung wrote, "and the less it is embodied in the individual's conscious life, the blacker and denser it is."[2]

The shadow is therefore anything we can't or won't see about ourselves, the aspects of ourselves we feel so deeply ashamed of that we hide them from ourselves and others. We have an extraordinary capacity for self-deception, so our shadows are often well-hidden—and yet they have great power over our thoughts and behaviors.

Although we cannot see our shadows, they give us clues about themselves. Any time we react strongly to something, in a way that's disproportionate to the circumstance, our shadows are likely shaping our reactions. A familiar example is when we feel righteous indignation about something and have a burning need to rant about it to someone who will agree with us; a strong but unexpressed aspect of ourselves has found an outlet valve.

Religion can be a tool for keeping the shadow hidden—but it cannot destroy the shadow. Instead, it often serves to make the shadow even more dangerously powerful. The very things that organized Christianity condemns as sins may also be the things we hide within our shadow. The church's disapproval puts even more pressure on us to keep those things hidden.

Facing our shadows challenges us to investigate what underlies our "good" actions. Maybe we've followed the rules because of fear or pride or wanting to be seen as good. Anything we do for show is securing our descriptive self, while masking something we think we need to hide.

Because we are not very conscious of the shadow, it tends to respond in an instinctive and irrational way, leaving us feeling out of control of some of our responses. Most of us have had the experience where something nasty pops up in our minds (or out of our mouths) and we think, "Wow, where did that come from?"

This lack of awareness of our shadows also leads to projections, where we turn a sense of our own inferiority into a moral deficiency in someone else. The more critical we are of others, the more this shows us we have unacknowledged areas in ourselves we are not facing. These projections insulate and cripple us by forming an ever-thicker fog of illusion between ourselves and the real world. We see this illustrated throughout history; the Spanish Inquisition, Nazism, violence against women, apartheid, and gay-bashing are just a few examples of people so convinced of the moral righteousness of their cause they were unable to recognize the hatefulness and evil of their own actions. These are extreme examples, but we all have this tendency within us. It shows up whenever we point the finger of blame at anybody for whatever reason.

The power of the shadow is further reinforced when we create self-justifying storylines to excuse ourselves and maintain our positions of power and righteousness. These stories have become so habitual that we often don't even notice them, and they are very difficult to let go. They keep us even more tethered to our shadow-responses to life. Some examples of these are: "Well, they had it coming!" or "I couldn't help it, they made me do it." Or one I tend to use a lot: "I'm allowed to be critical of them because they are so critical of other people." These storylines can lead to behavior that escalates until it is out of control.

Working with the Shadow

We begin by gradually recognizing the persona we show to the world, the image we like to project. We need to be especially careful of identifying with any idealized role or self-image, such as that of a spiritual leader, provider, mother, good wife, doctor, nice person, professor, moral believer, or some kind of leadership role. The more we are attached to these self-images, the more shadow self we are likely to have. We need to carefully observe our "good" or "righteous" attitudes and behaviors, since all of these reinforce our idealized self-image and are a clue that our true motives need to be recognized.

We also need to become aware of the parts of ourselves we have kept well-hidden, which all too often control us. This requires observing ourselves and our responses to life. When we see an over-reaction, this is a clue that something unexpressed is behind that reaction. We can begin to probe this gently, and hold it open as a question. "What am I trying to protect? What am I frightened of?"

As we observe ourselves, a heavy-handed, critical attitude is not helpful. If we beat ourselves up in the process of looking at our shadows, then we are likely to suppress something else, creating still another shadow problem for ourselves. Instead, we need to take ourselves lightly, learning to chuckle at ourselves when we see our silly over-reactions, while bringing a gentle self-compassion to the difficult areas we encounter.

As we watch our thought patterns, we will begin to notice the voices in our heads that continually narrate our lives, often using self-justifying storylines or reinterpreting our motives in such a way that they sound moral or selfless. When we recognize these narratives, we may want to ask: *What is really going on inside? What are my true motives?* This level of self-awareness is crucial if we are to have any kind of freedom from our shadow-selves. Again, the point is to not castigate ourselves but to learn to lightly let go of the storylines and the sense of identity they carry.

The shadow is not evil, just hidden and repressed. It's not distasteful, and it doesn't need to be surgically removed. It is merely our very wise unconscious telling us, "Hey, this is a part of yourself you're neglecting." The shadow is a part of ourselves we are not listening to, and so it becomes more forceful and sometimes even shocking. Very often the unconscious is simply striving for more balance in our lives—for example, if we try to deny our sexuality, this may come out forcefully in the form of shadow; or if we try to be someone who never gets angry, our shadows may come out in aggressive or passive-aggressive ways. The unconscious is simply striving for us to be the most complete versions of ourselves we can be. By not recognizing our imbalance or shadow, we may end up doing harm—but as we recognize and integrate the shadow into our full selves, it becomes a gift to us. The shadow sides of ourselves may seem overwhelmingly powerful, aggressive, and repulsive when caged, but often, when acknowledged and accepted, the shadow is a surprisingly gentle force, simply striving for balance and holistic well-being.

The more we face and acknowledge the things in ourselves that don't fit into our perfect image of ourselves, the more our idealized, false image is diminished. In this way we become more in touch with our true selves, our unique identities "hidden with Christ in God." As we understand the shadow, we can integrate it, reincorporating the shadow into the whole of us, which produces a stronger, more spacious sense of self that offers more space and acceptance to others, giving them room to also grow and expand.

Shadow work allows us to discover true, deep, and lasting freedom from the things that tether and control us. If we don't recognize and integrate our shadows, however, they will keep dictating our instinctive, irrational responses to life. We will continue to project our insecurities onto others, while becoming more and more judgmental and cramped inside.

But God's faithfulness to us means the Spirit will lead us into these shadowlands, where we are faced with the full horror of who we are. This is painful and humiliating. Facing our shadows takes enormous courage and strength. There is nowhere to hide, and the road often feels narrow and lonely.

But this is the messy narrowness of the birth canal that leads to new life! God is faithfully tending our souls, bringing to light that which has been hidden, and using it to bring us to full maturity and freedom. Throughout this journey, we are assured of God's presence with us, guiding us with tenderness, wisdom, and love. The psalmist knew this when he wrote, "Even though I walk through the valley of the shadow of death, I will fear no evil, for you are with me; your rod and your staff, they comfort me" (Psalm 23:4).

Peter's Shadow

We see an example of how Jesus handled the shadow in his interactions with his disciple, Simon Peter. Peter believed he was strong, reliable, and dependable. His belief in his descriptive self was so strong that he tried to convince Jesus to believe in it too. When Jesus told his disciples that they would all abandon him, Peter answered, "Even if all fall away, I will not."

> "I tell you the truth," Jesus answered, "today—yes, tonight—before the rooster crows twice you yourself will disown me three times."
>
> But Peter insisted emphatically, "Even if I have to die with you, I will never disown you." (Mark 14:27–31)

I don't think Peter was consciously being deceptive with his grand claims; he really seemed to believe this about himself. This is why the shadow can be so powerful—we often don't even know it's there! Just a short while later, though, when Peter was in a tense situation where he actually had to follow through on his promises, his idealized self crumbled.

> Then seizing [Jesus], they led him away and took him into the house of the high priest. Peter followed at a distance. And when some there had kindled a fire in the middle of the courtyard and had sat down together, Peter sat down with them. A servant girl saw him seated there in the firelight. She looked closely at him and said, "This man was with him."
>
> But he denied it. "Woman, I don't know him," he said.
>
> A little later someone else saw him and said, "You also are one of them."
>
> "Man, I am not!" Peter replied.
>
> About an hour later another asserted, "Certainly this fellow was with him, for he is a Galilean."
>
> Peter replied, "Man, I don't know what you're talking about!"
>
> Just as he was speaking, the rooster crowed. The Lord turned and looked straight at Peter. Then Peter remembered the word the Lord had spoken to him:

"Before the rooster crows today, you will disown me three times." And he went outside and wept bitterly. (Luke 22:54–62)

Peter had tried making good on his promise by following Jesus at a distance. As soon as he was really under pressure, though, he couldn't keep this up. His fear and lack of courage were parts of himself he had tried so hard to hide, from himself and others, that he had actually believed in his own bravado. In this moment, however, his hidden weaknesses took over, and he was forced to face the shadow side of himself. He must have felt devastated by what he saw in himself, especially in the light of his earlier grand promises. Now, he faced the full horror of himself; he could no longer hide behind his swaggering persona.

When Jesus turned and looked straight at Peter, my sense is that this was not a look of accusation as much as of recognition. Peter had been unmasked; he had nowhere to hide from the full truth of himself. His idealized self had been stripped away. No wonder he wept bitterly.

John's Gospel continues Peter's story a few days later:

Afterward Jesus appeared again to his disciples, by the Sea of Galilee. It happened this way: Simon Peter, Thomas, Nathanael, the sons of Zebedee, and two other disciples were together.

"I'm going out to fish," Simon Peter told them, and they said, "We'll go with you."

So they went out and got into the boat, but that night they caught nothing. Early in the morning, Jesus stood on the shore, but the disciples did not realize that it was Jesus. He called out to them, "Friends, haven't you any fish?"

"No," they answered.

He said, "Throw your net on the right side of the boat and you will find some."

When they did, they were unable to haul the net in because of the large number of fish. (John 21:1–6)

Apparently, Peter had decided to go back to his old identity as a fisherman. My sense is that Peter's identity as a successful disciple of Jesus had been dismantled, so he was returning to a trustworthy old identity, something he thought he could rely on. Instead, he failed even at this; he and his friends had been fishing all night and had caught nothing. So here we see Peter stripped not only of his identity as the best follower of Jesus but also as a successful fisherman.

The part I love most in this story is how Jesus handled Peter after they had breakfast on the beach.

When they had finished eating, Jesus said to Simon Peter, "Simon son of John, do you love me more than these?"

"Yes, Lord," he said, "you know that I love you."

Jesus said, "Feed my lambs."

Again Jesus said, "Simon son of John, do you love me?"

He answered, "Yes, Lord, you know that I love you."

Jesus said, "Take care of my sheep."

The third time he said to him, "Simon son of John, do you love me?"

Peter was hurt because Jesus asked him the third time, "Do you love me?" He said, "Lord, you know all things; you know that I love you."

Jesus said, "Feed my sheep. Very truly I tell you, when you were younger you dressed yourself and went where you wanted; but when you are old you will stretch out your hands, and someone else will dress you and lead you where you do not want to go." (John 21:15–18)

The first time Jesus asked the question "Do you love me?" the Greek word used is *agape*, which means Divine, self-giving love that would lay down one's life for another. This echoed the earlier claim Peter made, that he would follow Jesus to the point of death. When Jesus asked Peter, "Do you love me more than these?" most commentators believe Jesus was referring to Peter's identity as a fisherman—the nets, boat, the catch, and the way of life itself. When Peter replied, however, he used the Greek *fileo*, which refers to a friendship kind of love.

The second time Jesus asked the question, he again used the word *agape*, but without the "more than these" phrase. It's a question that asked a little less of Peter, implying, "Okay, you don't love me more than you love your identity as a fisherman— but do you love me enough to lay down your life for me?" Again Peter answered with the word *fileo*. In these responses, it seems Peter had let go of his grandiosity and was a bit more in touch with the reality of his limitations. Never once did he reply with the word *agape*, which would have been the grand lay-down-my-life claim. Instead, he replied with the more down-to-earth, honest response.

The third time Jesus asked the question, "Do you love me?" he too used the word *fileo*, and here he seems to be asking Peter, "Do you even love me as a friend?" This must have been a hard question for Peter to hear; not only had he failed Jesus as a disciple but also as a friend.

The text mentions that Jesus asked this question three times, providing a clear link with the number of times Peter denied him. Jesus' queries were not asked in an accusatory way; they simply expressed Jesus' recognition of reality, while inviting Peter into a more honest, vulnerable awareness of who he was. Jesus didn't offer "cheap grace" by sweeping Peter's behavior under the carpet; he did not let Peter pretend he never denied Jesus, but he invited Peter to recognize his shadow side while in a relational space of deep and profound grace. This is grace that does not leave us stuck in our illusions and knee-jerk patterns; instead, it shines the light on reality and offers us a way through the shadow valleys into truth and freedom.

Peter had to come to the end of his illusions about his own heroism and greatness. He had been through a crisis of facing his limitations, and his idealized self had been dismantled. It was only through this process of honestly facing and then surrendering the false image—in dying to his self-constructed identity as the greatest, mightiest apostle—that he could discover the full meaning of grace and fall into the true identity of who he was in God.

Our deeper identities in God are unshakable, because they do not depend on circumstance or others' opinions or our own efforts. They are sheer gifts from God that have been there all along, deep within us. Our awareness of them grows, however, as we become disillusioned with the personas we present to the world.

Notice that each time Peter affirms his love of Jesus, Jesus tells him, "Feed my sheep." When we operate out of our deeper true-self identities, rooted in God and connected to Jesus as the vine that gives us life, we are able to also nourish others spiritually. If, however, we operate from our self-constructed identities, we will just be part of the problem, no matter how worthy our actions. As Jesus said, "If you remain in me and I in you, you will bear much fruit; apart from me you can do nothing" (John 15:5).

Shadows and Wells

The interaction between Jesus and the woman at the well, as told in the Gospel of John, gives us another example of how Jesus addressed the shadow. The story starts like this:

> [Jesus] left Judea and went back once more to Galilee. Now he had to go through Samaria. So he came to a town in Samaria . . . and Jesus, tired as he was from the journey, sat down by the well. It was about noon.
>
> When a Samaritan woman came to draw water, Jesus said to her, "Will you give me a drink?" (His disciples had gone into the town to buy food.) (John 4:3–8)

The details included in this story tell us quite a lot about the woman's circumstances. Customarily, women drew water in groups, in the early morning when it was still cool. The fact that this woman was at the well by herself, and that she had to come there at noon, after the other women had finished drawing water, implies she was socially ostracized. She was a woman rejected by other women, perhaps because of her lifestyle. Jesus would have known all this when he approached her.

Good Jewish men did not talk with women. Women were seen as potential sources of uncleanness, and men were advised to avoid all contact with them except for what was necessary for the procreation of children. Samaritan women were seen as being even more unclean; according to some Jewish teachings of the day, Samaritan women began menstruating at birth, which made even little Samaritan girls unclean in Jewish males' eyes.[3] Since all it took for a man to become ritually unclean was to interact with someone unclean, when Jesus engaged in a conversation with a Samaritan woman, he made himself unclean by Jewish standards.

Jesus not only crossed religious and social barriers to speak to this Samaritan woman; he also crossed lines drawn by ethnic prejudice. The conflict between the Jews and the Samaritans had been going on for more than five hundred years. The Jews considered the Samaritans half-breeds, since they were descendants of Jews who had intermarried with Gentile tribes. Although both groups worshipped the same God, they did so differently. A common Jewish proverb said, "A piece of bread given by a Samaritan is more unclean than the flesh of a pig." Jews referred to Samaritans as a "herd," rather than a "nation," and some Jews went so far as to pray daily that Samaritans would not be granted everlasting life.[4] Most Jews avoided traveling through Samaria, preferring to take two extra days to go around Samaria when journeying from Judea to Galilee. So here we see Jesus initiating a conversation with an ultimate outsider—a Samaritan, a woman, and one of the local community's outcasts.

> The Samaritan woman said to him, "You are a Jew and I am a Samaritan woman. How can you ask me for a drink?" (For Jews do not associate with Samaritans.)

Jesus answered her, "If you knew the gift of God and who it is that asks you for a drink, you would have asked him and he would have given you living water."

"Sir," the woman said, "you have nothing to draw with and the well is deep. Where can you get this living water? . . ."

Jesus answered, "Everyone who drinks this water will be thirsty again, but whoever drinks the water I give them will never thirst. Indeed, the water I give them will become in them a spring of water welling up to eternal life."

The woman said to him, "Sir, give me this water so that I won't get thirsty and have to keep coming here to draw water."

He told her, "Go, call your husband and come back."

"I have no husband," she replied.

Jesus said to her, "You are right when you say you have no husband. The fact is, you have had five husbands, and the man you now have is not your husband. What you have just said is quite true."(John 4:9–11, 13–18)

The woman gave an evasive answer typical of someone who is ashamed and hiding something. Many of us can probably relate to this, for we too cover over our real stories with half-truths, while we fail to disclose certain key elements of our lives.

Jesus encountered this woman's shadow, a part of herself she was keeping hidden. Women of Jesus' day did not have the choice to divorce their husbands; only men could divorce their wives. This means that this woman had been left by five husbands who had either died or become tired of her. Her life had been extremely painful—and then she had been ostracized for it, her dignity utterly stripped away. Jesus didn't scold her for hiding the facts but merely confronted her with the truth, in a gentle, matter-of-fact, even humorous way. My sense is that Jesus was saying to her: "I see you. I know who you are, the pain and rejection you've been through. I know why others reject you, but you don't need to hide from me. I see you and I love you."

The woman is impressed by Jesus but still confused.

> "Sir," the woman said, "I can see that you are a prophet. Our ancestors worshipped on this mountain, but you Jews claim that the place where we must worship is in Jerusalem."
>
> "Woman," Jesus replied, "believe me, a time is coming when you will worship the Father neither on this mountain nor in Jerusalem. . . . . Yet a time is coming and has now come when the true worshippers will worship the Father in the Spirit and in truth, for they are the kind of worshippers the Father seeks. God is spirit, and his worshippers must worship in the Spirit and in truth."

The woman said, "I know that Messiah" (called Christ) "is coming. When he comes, he will explain everything to us."

Then Jesus declared, "I, the one speaking to you—I am he." . . .

Many of the Samaritans from that town believed in him because of the woman's testimony, "He told me everything I ever did." So when the Samaritans came to him, they urged him to stay with them, and he stayed two days. And because of his words many more became believers. (John 4:19–21, 23–26, 39–41)

The woman's interaction with Jesus enabled her to find a new confidence and inner authority, to the extent that people who had previously treated her as an outsider believed her account of Jesus before they had even met him. This remarkable authority resulted in a complete social shift as far as this woman was concerned. She was the person who brought the Messiah to the village. She became a spiritual leader in her community, and we see streams of living water flowing from within her to the others in her village.

But first, she had been seen for who she was, in all her painful reality with her hidden parts unmasked—and then Jesus had accepted her and loved her unconditionally. Richard Rohr has written about this deeply transformative experience:

This is the way that God seduces us all into the economy of grace—by loving us in spite of ourselves in the very places where we cannot, or will not, or dare not love ourselves. God shocks and stuns us into love. *God does not love us if we change; God loves us so that we can change.*[5]

Notice that in Jesus' conversation with the Samaritan woman, when he described the relationship God wants with us, he referred to both Spirit and truth (vs. 23). "Spirit" tells us that the Life-Giver is not confined to a sacred place or time, or to a special group; the Divine is fully accessible and available to everyone, everywhere, as the Hebrew scriptures promised: "I will pour out my Spirit on all people" (Joel 2:28). But what did Jesus mean when he spoke of worshipping God "in truth"?

Brought up in an evangelical belief system, I used to think that when Jesus referred to "truth" in this story, he was telling us we need to get our belief system "right." I've come to realize, though, that Jesus was speaking about honesty and realness, rather than anything doctrinal. The Greek word used here is *aléthinos,* which means "true" in the sense of "real, genuine." The word emphasizes an organic connection between external behaviors and their under-lying source; it contrasts reality against that which is counterfeit or merely pretended. In other words, true worship means being real in our relationship with God, opening ourselves so the Beloved can see us as we really are, and so that we can receive unconditional love and acceptance. Streams of living water will then flow from us to others, because the channel that connects us with the Source has been opened.

This Source of living water is within each of us, the "Christ in you, the hope of glory" (Colossians 1.27). It is already there, and it has always been there, but we clog it with our masking, faking, and hiding. When we allow ourselves to be seen for who we are, however, letting go of our protective, socially acceptable facades, our simplistic doctrinal assumptions and pat answers, our ego-driven pretensions—and finally, when we accept that we are God's beloved—then the spring of life-water within us is free to flow, into our consciousness and out into the world.

Some of the steps in the Alcoholics Anonymous Twelve-Step program[6] relate directly to this shadow work:

> We admitted we were powerless over alcohol—that our lives had become unmanageable. (Step 1)

> We made a searching and fearless moral inventory of ourselves. (Step 4)

> We admitted to God, to ourselves, and to another human being the exact nature of our wrongs. (Step 5)

In reference to Step 4, Richard Rohr wrote:

> Moral scrutiny is not to discover how good or bad I am and regain some moral high ground, but it is to begin

some honest "shadow boxing" which is at the heart of all spiritual awakening. Yes, "the truth will set you free" as Jesus says; "but first it will make you miserable," as many others have said. . . . [It is] the necessary sadness and humiliation that comes from seeing one's own failures and weaknesses. Without confidence in a Greater Love, none of us will have the courage to go inside. . . . People only come to deeper consciousness by intentional struggles with contradictions, conflicts, inconsistencies, inner confusions, and what the biblical tradition calls "sin" or moral failure. The goal is actually not the perfect avoidance of all sin, which is not possible, but the struggle itself, and the encounter and wisdom that comes from it. God brings us—through failure—from unconsciousness to ever-deeper consciousness and conscience.[7]

The fifth step, admitting our wrongs to another human being, reminds us that removing our masks is not just a me-and-my-God private thing. We cannot show our real selves to God while keeping up our pretenses with each other. Confronting our shadows is work done both internally and externally, and the role of community is important. The feedback we receive from others, showing us what we can't see about ourselves, can help us see more deeply into our shadows.

Unmasking ourselves doesn't mean we have to show everything to everybody, though. We need healthy boundaries, and we need to protect ourselves from the bullies of society, including, sometimes, the church. But we do need to be known and seen by a few close and trusted people, and trusted faith communities and other groups can offer support and feedback. When feedback is modeled on the love, gentleness, and acceptance of Jesus, our friendships and spiritual communities become powerful opportunities for transformation, healing, and hope, not only for ourselves but for the larger world. This is what Jesus meant when he spoke of streams of living water.

And so, we need to hear the gentle voice of God and one another saying, "I see you in all your shame and struggles. I see you as you are, with all your triumphs and defeats, in your hope and despair. You no longer need to hide from me." And then, with our dignity restored by love, we will hear God say:

> *See, I am doing a new thing!*
> *Now it springs up; do you not perceive it?*
> *I am making a way in the wilderness*
> *and streams in the wasteland.*

—Isaiah 43:19

INVITATION TO REFLECT

Spend a while sitting still and focusing gently on your breathing, allowing yourself to become quiet inside.

Then take some time to consider: have you become aware of any areas in your life that have been hidden or unacknowledged? Make a note of these in your journal.

Now ask yourself:

- What are the fears associated with these hidden areas?

- How would it feel to share these with trusted friends or a spiritual companion?

- What is your sense of God's response as you acknowledge these hidden areas? As you face them, can you allow yourself to be gathered into a tender relational space with God?

Express your honest response to God in whatever way is most real for you.

Finally, allow yourself to become quiet again, remaining still, open, and receptive to God for a few minutes.

NOTES

1. Richard Rohr. *Falling Upward: A Spirituality for the Two Halves of Life* (Hoboken, NJ: Wiley, 2011), p. 131.

2. Carl Jung. *The Wisdom of Carl Jung,* Edward Hoffman, ed. (New York: Citadel, 2003), p. 81.

3. Raymond E. Brown. *The Gospel According to John I-XII*, Anchor Bible Series, vol 29 (Garden City, NY: Doubleday, 1966), p. 170.

4. Ibid.

5. Richard Rohr. *Breathing Under Water: Spirituality and the Twelve Steps* (Cincinnati, OH: Franciscan Media, 2021), p. 40.

6. Alcoholics Anonymous. *Twelve Steps and Twelve Traditions* (New York: Alcoholics Anonymous World Services, 2013).

7. Rohr. *Breathing Under Water,* pp. 30–34.

PART VI

Transforming Our Pain

19

Suffering

Pain teaches a most counterintuitive thing:
we must go down before we even know what up is.
In terms of the ego, most religions teach in some way
that all must "die before they die."
Suffering of some sort seems to be
the only thing strong enough to both destabilize
and reveal our arrogance, our separateness,
and our lack of compassion.

−RICHARD ROHR[1]

Suffering can be transformed into a contemplative practice. Unlike other practices, however, we cannot plan for it or set aside time for it on a daily basis. Instead, this contemplative practice is our approach to the suffering that already comes our way.

We grow up with the belief that good people shouldn't suffer, and that if we do suffer, it is because we have done something wrong. We either believe God is punishing us, or that we are not getting things quite right in our way of living and need to make adjustments. In reality, though, no matter how well we try to live, the nature of life involves suffering. People get sick, accidents happen, and things go wrong. Time itself brings loss: circumstances and people change, as do our bodies, and we may perceive these changes as painful losses. We try to make sense of it, sometimes by blaming ourselves, God, or others; we try to get some kind of control over events so we don't have to feel the pain. But this is all the work of the calculating mind, and in the end, it only produces more suffering. As we lock ourselves in ever-tightening habits of thinking and resistance, we become trapped in a cage of inner turmoil.

The Example of Job

The Book of Job is a poignant portrayal of the journey of suffering. Job was a good family man, successful and wealthy, but in very quick succession, he lost his possessions, his children, and his health. At first, he got caught in the usual human reactions of despair, even longing for death, as conveyed in these verses:

> Why did I not perish at birth, and die as I came from the womb? Why were there knees to receive me and breasts that I might be nursed? For now I would be lying down

in peace; I would be asleep and at rest. . . . Why is light given to those in misery, and life to the bitter of soul, to those who long for death that does not come. . . ? Why is life given to a man whose way is hidden whom God has hedged in? For sighing has become my daily food; my groans pour out like water. What I feared has come upon me; what I dreaded has happened to me. I have no peace, no quietness; I have no rest, but only turmoil. (Job 3:11–13, 20–21, 23–26)

Job's friends tried to commiserate with him, but their counsel wasn't helpful. They questioned whether he or his children had done something to offend God and suggested that he needed to live a more righteous life. They were convinced there was something Job could do to rectify the situation and win back God's approval.

These are typical strategies of the calculating mind that can only think in logical sequences determined by cause-and-effect and dualistic good-versus-evil thinking. The ways of God and life, however, are infinitely beyond our capacity to understand with our rational minds. If we are honest with ourselves, we have to admit our finite minds simply cannot comprehend human suffering, especially the suffering of the innocent.

In the midst of Job's devastating suffering, however, a deep shift took place in him, and, as Cynthia Bourgeault wrote, "Job's faith and hope seem to grow stronger and stronger."

Far from being crushed, they take on a life of their own. As the agony of his ordeal settles into simply the way things are, and even the need to apportion blame and find coherence subsides, what seems to take wing in him is a single-hearted yearning to see God face to face. . . . In one of the most extraordinary passages ever written, Job sits destitute amid the wreckage of what was once his life, and sings: "I know that my Redeemer lives, and that in the end he will stand upon the earth. And after my skin has been destroyed, yet in my flesh I will see God."[2]

This is what James Finley described as the axial moment—the moment when someone moves from being defined by their pain to deeper openness and trust.[3]

Suffering and Spiritual Growth

As we see in Job's story, suffering plays an important role in our journeys into God. It challenges the formulas we carry in our calculating minds, forcing us to let go of our habitual ways of seeing life. When our fairy-tale endings just don't work out as we had hoped, or when life seems to be a chaotic, unfathomable mess, we have the opportunity to open to a deeper dimension of life, a deeper relationship with God, and a way of knowing beyond our minds' reasoning capacity.

Suffering also dismantles our illusions about ourselves, showing us the inadequacy of the identities we try so hard to defend and protect. Only as we recognize and let go of our self-made identities can we experience the contemplative way of knowing who we are in God, our unshakable identities that are rooted and established in love. Ultimately, as Job's story so beautifully depicts, suffering opens in us a yearning ache for God that peaceful, easy times never do.

Another story that reveals suffering's spiritual dimension is the journey of the two people on the road to Emmaus, as told in the Gospel of Luke (24:13–35). The two disciples in this story had a clear mental picture of who Jesus was: "We had hoped that he was the one to redeem Israel," they explained (verse 21). But now Jesus was dead, and these two people were left with the shattered pieces of their beliefs and hopes. This suffering was necessary, however, so that they could begin to recognize and let go of their assumptions about what redemption should look like. With their expectations destroyed, they could open to the deeper reality of Christ's presence with them.

This awakening to the presence of God with us, even within the midst of the chaos and upheaval of life-as-it-is, opens us to the contemplative dimension of life. In this depth dimension, we intuit (rather than know with rational certainty) that God is intimately present with us, within us, in every moment of our lives. This is not a knowing our minds can grasp; instead, it is a knowing we live into as we release our minds' expectations and assumptions.

Working with Our Suffering

As we begin to work with our suffering, we need to remember our humanity; encountering suffering in a new way has to be undertaken with patience, gentleness, and self-compassion. Expecting ourselves to dive into our suffering places and come up triumphant would be hubris (excessive spiritual pride), which is just another manifestation of ego. We have to tread lightly as we approach the flame of our suffering.

The first step is to see suffering for what it is, rather than shying away from its reality or distracting ourselves with entertainment, substances, or other avoidance strategies. This is so much easier said than done, especially in our modern-day lives, where we have an endless array of sparkly distractions just waiting for us to push a button and be entertained. The more we avoid our suffering, however, the deeper it will eat away at us. No wonder then that as our lives get more and more filled with instant bright bling, the rate of depression and substance abuse increases!

The second step is to recognize and release our minds' attempts to understand or fix our circumstances. We also need to surrender our habits of wrapping self-absorbed narratives around the suffering; these only serve to fuel the flame of inner pain.

Third, we need to practice accepting the circumstances rather than resisting them, which only makes the suffering worse. We can instead choose to soften and open to what is happening. (The

Welcoming Prayer in chapter 14 can be a powerful tool to help us do this.)

Finally, we allow ourselves to become intimate with the suffering within us. We listen to it, gently and respectfully, gradually becoming more familiar with its felt texture. As we do this, we awaken to the presence of Christ, who is intimately with us when we are in pain.

The cross is a powerful symbol that shows us that suffering belongs in our spiritual journeys. We realize that Christ's wounds and our wounds, individually and communally, are mysteriously interwoven. This allows an intimate sense of our union with God and one another, one we would not have access to without the experience of suffering. As we dare to venture into the abyss-like places of our pain, we discover the portal that opens from these depths into the mystery of infinite Love, the unshakable, holding, grounding presence of God. The very suffering we had tried to avoid ultimately gives us access to the awareness of "Christ in us, the hope of glory" (Colossians 1:27). As Richard Rohr described,

> We can then see our own suffering as a voluntary participation in the one Great Sadness of God (Colossians 1:24). Within this meaningful worldview, we can build something new, good, and forever original, while neither playing the victim nor making victims of others. We can be free conduits of grace into the world.[4]

A poem by Rashani Rea describes the possibilities that can emerge from our suffering and brokenness:

> There is a brokenness
> out of which comes the unbroken,
> a shatteredness out of which blooms the unshatterable.
> There is a sorrow
> beyond all grief which leads to joy
> and a fragility out of whose depths emerges strength.
> There is a hollow space too vast for words
> through which we pass with each loss,
> out of whose darkness we are sanctioned into being.
> There is a cry deeper than all sound
> whose serrated edges cut the heart
> as we break open
> to the place inside which is unbreakable
> and whole,
> while learning to sing.[5]

Suffering can be a portal into the spacious realm of contemplative knowing, "which is unbreakable and whole," so that we can say with Job, with a gut-deep knowing far deeper than any intellectual certainty, "I know that my Redeemer lives. . . . And after my skin has been destroyed, yet in my flesh I will see God."

The dance of life finds its beginnings in grief. . . .
Here a completely new way of living is revealed.
It is the way in which pain can be embraced,
not out of a desire to suffer,
but in the knowledge that something new
will be born in the pain.

—HENRI NOUWEN[6]

INVITATION TO REFLECT

Spend a while sitting still and focusing gently on your breathing, allowing yourself to become quiet inside

Then ask yourself:

- As you were reading this chapter, did you become aware of any areas of suffering in your life you have not previously acknowledged? Make a note of these in your journal.

- What have been your usual responses to suffering? Have you tried to resist or shy away from pain? Have you distracted yourself so you don't have to experience it?

- What stories have you told yourself (and others) about your suffering?

- What does it feel like to let go of the stories, while remaining present to the suffering?

As emotions arise, imagine how you would respond to a child who was experiencing these feelings. Give yourself the same kind of care.

Now allow yourself to become quiet again, remaining still, open, and receptive to God for a few minutes.

NOTES

1. Richard Rohr. "Transforming Our Pain" from his Daily Meditations (February 26, 2016), https://cac.org/daily-meditations/.

2. Cynthia Bourgeault. *Mystical Hope: Trusting in the Mercy of God* (Lanham, MD: Cowley, 2001).

3. Carolyn Myss and James Finley. *Transforming Trauma: A Seven-Step Process for Spiritual Healing* (Louisville, CO: Sounds True, 2009).

4. Rohr.

5. Rashani. "The Unbroken" (1991), http://rashani.com/arts/poems/poems-by-rashani/the-unbroken/.

6. Henri J. M. Nouwen. *The Dance of Life: Weaving Sorrows and Blessings into One* (Notre Dame, IN: Ave Marie, 2006), p. 26.

20

Woundedness

Nobody escapes being wounded.
We are all wounded people,
whether physically, emotionally, mentally, or spiritually.
The main question is not, "How can we hide our wounds?"
so we don't have to be embarrassed, but
"How can we put our woundedness in the service of others?"
When our wounds cease to be a source of shame,
and become a source of healing,
we have become wounded healers.

—HENRI NOUWEN[1]

saiah wrote, "by his wounds we are healed" (53:5). I used to think
this meant that because Jesus suffered on the cross, I didn't have
to be wounded anymore; in other words, I could avoid the dark
places of unresolved inner pain. So I was bitterly disappointed when

I discovered my wounds have been stalking me throughout my life, no matter how hard I tried to believe in Jesus and no matter how fervently I prayed for healing or tried to wish my wounds away.

I have come to realize this verse is not referring to a magical healing but rather an invitation to journey into our wounded places—and there, within the context of our wounds, find healing. James Finley called this "the freedom from the tyranny of suffering in the midst of suffering."[2] He explained this more fully:

> The secret opening through which we pass into wholeness is hidden in the center of the wound we do not want to go near. The door that grants access to boundaryless fulfillment is hidden in the unfinished business of our lives; the things we do not want to get vulnerable about, the things we tend not to sit with and listen to.[3]

Without venturing into our wounded and hurting places, we will not discover the healing we so desperately long for.

Identifying Our Wounds

Sometimes, we find ourselves making choices that seem completely irrational, that contradict what we consider to be our core values, that make us feel ashamed or exposed. Or somebody says something that reduces us to a quivering wreck, paralyzes us, or enrages us way beyond proportion. We wonder if we are completely losing it, and we appear, even to ourselves, to be temporarily insane. Occasions like these give us clues that a trip switch in us has been triggered. We are reacting unconsciously to protect ourselves or to hide what we fear the most in ourselves.

Since we are often unaware of the deeper reasons that fuel our reactions, we may be blind to how extreme our responses are—but beneath all these reactive actions is a wound, usually grounded in a primal fear. It could be the fear of failure, the fear of rejection, the fear of punishment or harm, the fear of betrayal, the fear of loss, or the fear of missing out—or the fear of any number of other things.

The Danger of Self-Abandonment

Often we are ashamed of our wounds, and so we reject these parts of ourselves, abandoning them like unwanted orphans. When we don't recognize these wounded, abandoned places within us, we tend to fall into unhealthy behavior patterns. We numb ourselves in various ways—through compulsive activity, noise, gossip, dishonesty, escapism, entertainment, eating, working, and so on. These patterns are destructive, not only to ourselves but also to those we interact with, because they lock us into our automatic compulsions. When we respond from the true, authentic, and alive place where we are rooted in God, this in turn gives room for others to respond more freely—but instead, we often engage in strange dances of alternating defensiveness and retreat.

"We have a deeply ingrained propensity to recoil from our own brokenness, to judge it and loathe it," Martin Laird wrote.

"In doing this we avoid what God in Christ draws close to and embraces."[4] Thomas Merton put it like this:

> The Christ we find in ourselves is not identified with what
> we vainly seek to admire and idolize in ourselves—on the
> contrary, he has identified himself with what we resent in
> ourselves, for he has taken upon himself our wretchedness
> and our misery, our poverty and our sins.[5]

Growing up, I learned to be critical of myself. I even thought this was what God expected. I have come to realize, though, how damaging this attitude is. In the same way that a neglected child often grows up to be needy and destructive, the neglected parts in us become destructive to ourselves and others.

The author John Welwood used another metaphor—that of a haunted house—to describe this:

> Fleeing the raw, wounded places in ourselves because we
> don't think we can handle them is a form of self-rejection
> and self-abandonment that turns our feeling body into an
> abandoned, haunted house. The more we flee our shad-
> owy places, the more they fester in the dark and the more
> haunted this house becomes. And the more haunted it
> becomes, the more it terrifies us. This is a vicious circle
> that keeps us cut off from and afraid of ourselves. . . . We
> need to regard the wounded heart as a place of spiritual

practice. This kind of practice means engaging with our fears and vulnerabilities in a deliberate, conscious way.[6]

Working with Wounds as a Spiritual Practice

In order to interact with our wounds as a form of spiritual practice, we first have to learn to be present to these places. We consciously shift our habits of ignoring or wishing them away, and instead, we allow ourselves to be fully aware of them. When they arise, we let ourselves experience the emotions they trigger, and we feel how they manifest in our bodies.

We also stop weaving commentaries around our wounds, which can be worse than the wounds themselves, pulling us back into self-absorption and navel-gazing. One form of commentary might be embellishing on the wound with stories that say, "Look how wounded I am! Nobody else is as wounded as me." Or, "Nobody understands me, I'm so lonely," or, "My life is so hard." We also may be tempted to mentally relive the past or blame our parents for everything. We need to distinguish the difference between giving attention to the narratives our minds weave and being present with the wound itself.

When we allow ourselves to experience our emotions, as they are felt in our bodies, we discover they are not as bad as our imaginations built them up to be. We begin to sense a spaciousness around them that is larger and more grounding than the emotions themselves. As we do this in an attitude of prayer, in the Presence of God the Divine Therapist,[7] we open ourselves to God's compassion and unconditional acceptance.

Next, we have to learn acceptance and compassion for the places we have habitually rejected and scorned. As we show ourselves tender recognition, God's tenderness joins with ours and reaches into the same hurting places. God is always ready and yearning to do this, but we have to be the initiators, choosing to no longer reject our emotional orphans but to welcome them instead. We say "yes" to them as part of who we are.

When we approach our wounds from the perspective of our minds, however, we often think that in order to heal them, we must find a way to intellectually make sense of them. As Henri Nouwen wrote:

> It is better to feel your wounds deeply than to understand them, to let them into your silence. You need to let your wounds go down into your heart. Then you can live them through and discover that they will not destroy you. Your heart is greater than your wounds.[8]

As we become present to these places and open them to God, we will recognize what God sees: we are precious in our brokenness. We allow ourselves to receive the compassion we so desperately need.

This allows us to extend the same depth of compassion to others. In fact, this process is essential to our service to others, since it opens within us a grounded humility and gentle acceptance toward the wounded places in others. John Welwood wrote, "Relating to the full spectrum of our experience . . . leads to a self-acceptance that expands our capacity to embrace and accept others as well."[9] Henri Nouwen suggested that "when we become aware that we do not have to escape our pains, but that we can mobilize them into a common search for life, those very pains are transformed from expressions of despair into signs of hope."[10]

Contemplative prayer is another way to interact with the spiritual dimension of our wounds. As Martin Laird wrote, "The doorway into the silent land is a wound. Silence lays bare that wound."[11] Although we may begin a contemplative practice because we are seeking peace, we soon find that this form of prayer does not paint over our wounds with an easy but shallow serenity. Instead, it leads us into our wounds, where, Laird wrote, "we discover that our wound and the wound of God are one wound . . . human woundedness, brokenness, death itself are transformed from dead ends to doorways into Life."[12] And so the deeper we go in our prayer practice, the deeper we will be led into these wounded places, and there we discover an intimacy with the Wounded Healer we otherwise would never experience.

As we journey prayerfully into our wounded places, we enter what feels like a dark, bottomless abyss. There are no detours we can take around the valley of the shadow of death. We feel with Jesus his sense of abandonment, echoing his words on the cross: "My God, my God, why have you forsaken me?" (Matthew 27:46). But in this place of agony and lostness, we meet Jesus. We discover the very portal he entered in his own journey from death to resurrection. As Paul wrote in Romans: "For if we have been united with him in a death like his, we will certainly also be united with him in a resurrection like his" (6:5). Paradoxically, the deepest, darkest wounds we have carried so fearfully and shamefully can become the places of most profound healing for ourselves and others.

What I have found personally, in working with my wounds, is that my regular practices of centering prayer, retreats, quiet times in Nature, and sacred reading have not made my wounds go away (which was very disappointing at first)—but something else happened instead. These practices helped me establish a stable, quiet center where I know who I am in God at a level that is deeper and more spacious than my emotions. Now, I have a sense of assurance that I can return to this steady inner place when I need to be regrounded. And from this place of inner stability, I gather the strength I need to approach my wounds. Irrational waves of emotions may still overwhelm and engulf me sometimes, but when that happens, I know I need only return to my quiet, unshakeable center point.

As I approach these wounded places in myself, not telling myself stories about them (which is a strong temptation), but simply being present to the felt experience of them with tenderness and compassion, I experience a new and living intimacy with the wounded Christ. I feel the Divine Presence as a loving embrace that joins me as I hold and soothe my wounds, and I sense the tender and knowing gaze of the Beloved seeing the whole of me. I know I am precious to God; even the messy, painful spots are loved.

Our wounds run deep, but the tender love of God is infinitely deeper. This means that the deeper we venture into our painful places, the deeper will be our awareness of God's boundless love. Our spiritual roots grow and spread, grounding us in Divine love.

With this sense of deep-rooted safety, we can be a healing presence to others. We need not fear that our own wounds will make us too weak for this work; instead, they give us a depth of compassion and inner authority much more powerful than eloquent words. James Finley explained that this is the only way we can confront the world's violence and suffering—"with the tap-root of our heart grounded in this invincible love that utterly transcends the suffering, radiates out in it and empowers us to be present to it in a way that doesn't overwhelm us and destroy us."[13]

A key thing I've learned from all this is that I can trust whatever arises as God's gift to me, a potential teacher if I allow myself to be present with it. I used to think that as a "spiritual person," I should feel peaceful and connected—and if I wasn't, then something had gone wrong and I must fix it. Now, however, I realize that when something pushes my buttons and I feel outraged, despondent, lost, or injured, this is not a mistake or a punishment, but rather an opportunity to look behind those buttons, to find the wounded places that triggered my responses. All of life is God's faithfulness. Everything is "grist for the mill" of our awakening.[14]

> *In a futile attempt to erase our past,*
> *we deprive the community of our healing gift.*
> *If we conceal our wounds out of fear and shame,*
> *our inner darkness can neither be illuminated*
> *nor become a light for others. . . .*
> *The art of gentleness toward ourselves*
> *leads us to be gentle with others—*
> *and is a natural prerequisite*
> *for our presence to God in prayer.*
>
> —BRENDAN MANNING[15]

INVITATION TO REFLECT

Spend a while sitting still and focusing gently on your breathing, allowing yourself to become quiet inside.

As you have been reading this chapter, did you become aware of any core wounds in yourself, places that cause you to react in ways that feel irrational or out of proportion to the situation? Make a note of these in your journal.

Allow yourself to stay with the felt experience of the hurting places while being gently accepting and compassionate toward those places in yourself. You might find it helpful to use some physical gesture of self-soothing as you do this, like putting your hand on your heart or on the place where you feel the wound most intensely in your body. As you do this, allow yourself to be gathered into the tender embrace of God.

Respond to God in whatever way feels most expressive for you.

Finally, allow yourself to become quiet again, remaining still, open and receptive to God for a few minutes.

NOTES

1. Henri J. M. Nouwen. *The Wounded Healer: Ministry in Contemporary Society* (New York: Crown, 2013), p. 22.

2. James Finley. "Breathing God," interview with Tami Simon, *Insights at the Edge* (Louisville, CO: Sounds True, 2021), https://www.resources.soundstrue.com/transcript/james-finley-breathing-god/.

3. James Finley. "Finding Our Way Along the Healing Path," *mindGAINS*, https://mindgains.org/findingourway/.

4. Martin Laird. *Into the Silent Land: A Guide to Christian Contemplation* (New York: Oxford University Press, 2006), p. 120.

5. Thomas Merton. *The Monastic Journey* (Collegeville, MN: Cistercian Publications, 1992), p. 71.

6. John Welwood. "Intimate Relationship as a Spiritual Crucible," in *Right Here with You: Bringing Mindful Awareness Into Our Relationships*, Andrea Miller, ed. (Boulder, CO: Shambhala, 2011), p. 174.

7. "The Divine Therapist" is a phrase used by Thomas Keating, for example in his book *Intimacy with God: An Introduction to Centering Prayer* (Chestnut Ridge, NY: Crossroad, 2009).

8. Henri J. M. Nouwen. *You Are the Beloved: Daily Meditations for Spiritual Living* (New York: Crown, 2017), p. 309.

9. Welwood, p. 177.

10. Nouwen. *The Wounded Healer*, p. 93.

11. Laird, p. 117.

12. Ibid., p. 118.

13. James Finley, from a talk given at the Living School of Action and Contemplation.

14. Ram Das said, "These days I try to simply love everything that comes my way, whether animate or inanimate, pleasant or painful. I hope you too can learn to absorb life's ecstasies and distresses into your spiritual practice so they are just more grist for the mill." In *Grist for the Mill: Awakening to Oneness* (New York: HarperCollins, 2014).

15. Brennan Manning. *Abba's Child: The Cry of the Heart for Intimate Belonging* (Colorado Springs, CO: Navigators, 2015), p. 29.

PART VII

Flowing Outward

21

Love

I did not know what love was
until I encountered one that kept opening,
and opening, and opening.

—CHRISTIAN WIMAN[1]

Each of our lives is like a boat floating on the ocean. As we grow up, we learn to care for and be proud of our own boat, as well as the special fleet of boats that is our family, religion, race, culture, or whatever community that contributes to our personal sense of identity. We decorate our boats, care for them, and are given rewards for having the biggest, fastest, or prettiest boat. We enter our boats in races to prove which is the best. We invest in their safety and security features, protecting them from storms and marauders.

At some point, however, our boats develop leaks, and we realize they are made from impermanent materials that rot and decay. If we are honest with ourselves, we also have to admit that the reward we receive from praise is short-lived. We have a gnawing sense that our life should be about so much more than just keeping our boats afloat. At this point, many of us try to tape over the leaks with duct tape. We carry on with the pretense that our boats are fine.

To make ourselves feel better about our own boats, we point fingers at other peoples' boats, criticizing them and distancing ourselves from them. In doing this, we try to convince ourselves that our boats are not only enough, but they are also better than everybody else's.

By the mercy of God, our boats' leaks eventually become so bad that we can't ignore them any longer. We may become desperate and despairing—or we may wake up to a larger reality. If we are able to engage wisely in this process, we allow ourselves to expand and deepen our sense of our identity beyond our single boat or even the fleet of boats to which we belong. We realize we are, in fact, part of the Ocean itself, the vast Ocean that holds and supports all beings, including a myriad other wondrous lifeforms we never knew existed when we were stuck in the small world of our little boat floating on the surface.

As we move deeper into this Ocean, we are submerged in more profound levels of peace and stillness than we knew were possible. If we hadn't surrendered our vested interest in our own little boat and the surrounding fleet of boats, we would never have encountered the supportive expanse that is spacious enough to compassionately hold the interests of all beings and lifeforms. This is the place of ultimate freedom. We no longer have to defend or promote our little boat-selves anymore. Now, we are part of something much vaster and more life-giving.

This analogy helps me understand love. As we are freed more and more from our selfish and separate interests, we open ourselves to God's self-giving, oceanic heart of love. From this boundless, generous place, we recognize the needs of others, and we reach out with love to touch their suffering. This love is not our own; it is flowing through us. As our sense of ourselves as separate and independent beings dissolves, we merge with the Heart of Love. We are a flowing-through of love, a participant in the work of love that is the pattern of all life.

Our world has many misguided notions about what love means. When we speak of God's love, we're not referring to a warm, fuzzy feeling of connection. The problem with equating love with *feeling* loved is that when we don't feel the connection, we assume love is not there. We worry we may have done something wrong that disconnected us from God. Only when we release our attachment to the feelings we equate with love can we experience the more subtle but all-pervasive depth of God's love, which underpins and infuses every moment of our lives.

We are no longer boats floating on the surface of the sea. Now we are like fish swimming in the ocean of love. As Catherine of Siena ıe soul is in God and God is in the soul, just as the fish is in ...ıd the sea in the fish."[2]

Love is also not an automatic response to an expression of neediness. This behavior has been termed "toxic charity,"[3] since it often strips the needy person of dignity and agency, while boosting our egos' needs to be the nice person, the hero or the savior figure.

Nor is love concerned with trying to solve all the social and political ills of our time. This is called *hubris* (excessive pride), and it's a thinly veiled egotistical belief that we can solve enormous problems using our calculating minds. Love, however, has to come from a much deeper place of consciousness than do our attempts to think our way to solutions. Real love is participation in Something and Someone much bigger than ourselves or our intellectual powers to come up with answers.

We cannot claim to love God at the expense of other people. Richard Rohr often repeats the phrase, "How you love anything is how you love everything." We cannot claim to love God while at the same time treating one another and the rest of creation with contempt or indifference. Our claim to love God must be consistent with our actions toward one another.

When a man asked Jesus what the most important commandment was, he answered:

> Love the Lord your God with all your heart and with
> all your soul and with all your mind and with all your

strength. . . . Love your neighbor as yourself. There is no commandment greater than these. (Mark 12:30–31)

Each time Jesus taught about love, he combined love of God and love of one another. And note that he said, "Love your neighbor *as yourself*"—in other words, "as if they are yourself, because they *are* your Self!"

All of us have bigger identities than the individual separate boats we think we are. We are all part of the Ocean. Jesus expressed this in his prayer for us:

That they may be one as we are one—I in them and you in me—so that they may be brought to complete unity. Then the world will know that you sent me and have loved them even as you have loved me. (John 17:22–23)

Awakening into the Heart of Love

This brings us to the crucial question of *how*. How do we participate with the Heart of Love? How does love become a contemplative practice?

A key to waking up from our individual identities and vested self-interests is to recognize the patterns that reinforce our sense of separate identities. Whenever we criticize or judge others, pointing out their failures or weaknesses or their "otherness" in some way, we are reinforcing the boundary lines of separation between us and them—and thereby strengthening the separate-self illusion that traps us. This is why Jesus taught so strongly about the danger of judging others (Matthew 7:1). A vital step, therefore, to awakening from the illusion of separateness is to become aware of our judgmental, critical behaviors.

This is not about merely avoiding obvious moral judgments. James Alison uses this wonderful analogy:

> For me [it] is like being at a huge and very spacious party at which there are an awful lot of people, most of whom are not at all like me, and with whom I don't have much in common. Furthermore this is a party to which I have been invited not because I'm special, but because the host invited me. If only I can let go of taking myself too seriously, then I'll get on with it and really enjoy the dance. One of the things about this party is that quite a lot of us spend quite a lot of time trying to work out who should be at the party and who shouldn't, even when the evidence is that the host is pretty promiscuous in his invitations.[4]

Alison goes on to describe how some people are self-appointed bouncers at the party, trying to exclude people for various reasons. The insidious temptation, however, can then be to bounce those bouncers, pointing fingers at those who are being judgmental as we say *they* don't belong at the party. Instead, we need to keep the dialogue open with everybody, no matter how much we disagree with their values and viewpoints. Real love challenges us to expand our sense of who is "in" and who is "out," so that *there are no outsiders*. Only then will we get a taste of the expansiveness of God's heart.

This leads us to another key in the contemplative practice of love: living each day with an attitude of openheartedness toward whomever we come into contact with. This is much easier said than done, but if we start each day with this intention, we will gradually find ourselves going deeper into the Ocean of God's love, where we recognize that other people are also part of the expansive Whole. We open our eyes to recognize Christ in others. As Jesus said, "Whatever you have done to the least of these, my brethren, you have done to me" (Matthew 25:40).

Jesus also expressed this with his teaching to love our enemies (Matthew 5:44). This is not the impossible moral command that it can seem at first glance, setting us up to fail. Rather, it is a wisdom practice that encourages us to identify where we use the label of "enemies" to separate ourselves from others. It breaks down the illusion of separation by building bridges of compassion with the ultimate "other."

Francis of Assisi taught:

Our Lord Jesus Christ himself, in whose footsteps we must follow, called the man who betrayed him his friend, and gave himself up of his own accord to his executioners. Therefore, our friends are those who for no reason cause us trouble and suffering, shame or injury, pain or torture, even martyrdom or death. It is these we must love, and love very much, because for all they do to us we are given eternal life.[5]

According to James Alison, Jesus invites us into a way of being that is "not in reaction in any way at all, but is purely creative, dynamic, outward going, and able to bring things into being and flourishing."[6]

Alison went on to say: "Living this out is going to look remarkably like a loss of identity, a certain form of death." We lose the clear definitions by which we have identified ourselves. It's all part of the process by which the powerful illusion of the separate self is gradually diminished.

Jesus concluded his teaching about enemies by saying, "Be perfect, therefore, as your heavenly Father is perfect" (Matthew 5:48). The Greek word translated as "perfect" is more accurately translated as "complete" or "whole"—in other words, undivided. We are invited to be spacious and open, not divided or constricted by being defined as separate from anybody. Ilia Delio described this as a form of loving that "is a consciousness of belonging to another, being part of the whole."

> To love is to be on the way toward integral wholeness, to live with an openness of mind and heart, to encounter the other—not as stranger—but as another part of oneself.

When we enter into the heart of love, that integral wholeness of love that is God, we enter into the field of relat-
edness. . . . This is the consciousness we need today, an
integral wholeness of love that is open to new life.[7]

An openhearted stance toward others also opens us to the flow
of God's love, allowing Divine love to be expressed through us. In
the words attributed to Francis of Assisi, we pray, "Lord, make me
an instrument of Your peace. Where there is hatred, let me sow love;
where there is injury, pardon. . . . Grant that I may not so much seek
to be consoled as to console; to be understood as to understand; to
be loved as to love; for it is in giving that we receive; . . . it is in dying
that we are born again to eternal life."

The love that flows through us from God challenges us to be
generous toward others, living lightly with our possessions. When a
rich young man came to Jesus, asking how he could have eternal life,
Jesus answered, "If you want to be perfect, go, sell your possessions
and give to the poor, and you will have treasure in heaven. Then
come, follow me" (Matthew 19:21). Here we see that same word,
perfect, and again it would be more accurately translated as "whole"
or "complete." By clutching our material possessions and placing
our own interests above others, we fossilize the boundaries around
our separate selves, reinforcing the old dead patterns of self-interest.
This not only keeps us stuck in restricted, unhappy ways of being but
also impedes the free flow the entire system needs to thrive and grow.

The more we think we have to lose, the harder it may be to let go of our possessions and boundary definitions. Later, in this same passage from Matthew, Jesus said that a camel can pass through the eye of a needle more easily than a wealthy person can enter the kingdom. This does not mean that rich people are unlikely to go to heaven; when Jesus spoke of "the kingdom," he was referring not to the afterlife but to the deeper way of being we've been describing throughout this book, a way of life that is intimately connected to the Giver of all life and love. It's not easy to allow ourselves to be stripped of our possessions and presumptions, all the things that interfere with our connection to the Life-Giver—but Jesus went on to say that although this may be impossible humanly speaking, "with God all things are possible" (Matthew 19:26).

The yearning that cries out from the cores of our beings is never satisfied by what we possess. When we try to go that route, focusing on our possessions, we end up frustrated, still empty; thinking to fill that emptiness with this world's riches, we only want more and more. But when we step away from the age-old game of accumulation and clinging, we realize it never worked. As we learn to live more lightly with our outward stuff, holding it with open hands instead of clenched fists, we soften and open our boundaries, allowing life and love to flow through us toward the needs of others. This is an aspect of what Jesus meant when he spoke of being connected to the vine (see John 15). Participation in the mystical body of Christ is another way to describe this way of Corinthians 12). Teresa of Avila expressed it this way:

> Christ has no body now but yours. No hands, no feet
> on earth but yours. Yours are the eyes through which he
> looks compassion on this world. Yours are the feet with
> which he walks to do good. Yours are the hands through
> which he blesses all the world. Yours are the hands, yours
> are the feet, yours are the eyes, you are his body. Christ
> has no body now on earth but yours.[8]

This love is pouring through us, but it is not self-generated. We are channels for the Source of Love, who is endlessly and generously pouring God-self out into the world.

Practices of openheartedness are essential to our journey deeper, supported by silent prayer or meditation, surrender, and presence, which progressively free us from our mind's illusions. As we deepen our awareness of the quiet, wordless expansive love of God, in whom we "live and move and have our being" (Acts 17:28), we discover the unique ways in which we each can participate in the work of the Spirit. We become coworkers with the Life-Giver, sharing the ongoing Divine labor to free humanity from the separation that leads to indifference, greed, violence, and prejudice.

We live in a world of grace,
and as we more consciously receive grace,
. . . each one of us becomes open to love
a little more completely,
and then love pours out of us and into the world.
As we become free, others experience freedom
in our presence and can choose to be open to love, too.
This is our life work, our great work,
that requires all that we have become
and all that we are becoming.

—JUDY CANNATO[9]

INVITATION TO PRACTICE

During the next few days, notice how you typically respond to the people with whom you live and work. Consider these questions:

- Do you see times when you judge people or keep them at a distance? How does this reinforce your sense of being a separate self?

- As you notice your typical responses, can you soften your boundaries to have a more openhearted attitude to others? How does this feel? How can you develop this into an ongoing practice?

Note your answers to these questions in your journal.

At the start of each day, you might find it helpful to set an intention for the day, for example, to be a channel for God's love and peace to flow through you into the lives of others. How does this change your attitude toward others? Does it shift your sense of self in any way?

NOTES

1. Christian Wiman. *My Bright Abyss: Meditation of a Modern Believer* (New York: Farrar, Straus and Giroux, 2013), p. 23.

2. Catherine of Siena, *The Dialogue* (Mahwah, NJ: Paulist Press, 1980), p. 27.

3. This phrase is used by Robert Lupton in his book *Toxic Charity: How Churches and Charities Hurt Those They Help (and How to Reverse It)* (New York: HarperCollins, 2012).

4. James Alison, *Undergoing God: Dispatches from the Scene of a Break-In* (New York: Continuum, 2006), pp. 166–172.

5. Francis of Assisi. "Rule of 1221," *St. Francis of Assisi: Omnibus of Sources* (Chicago, IL: Franciscan Herald Press, 1973), p. 47.

6. James Alison. *Love Your Enemy: Within a Divided Self,* essay available for download at www.jamesalison.co.uk/texts/eng50.html.

7. Ilia Delio. *The Unbearable Wholeness of Being: God, Evolution, and the Power of Love* (Maryknoll, NY: Orbis Books, 2013), p. xxv.

8. Teresa of Avila. In Roger Housden's *For Lovers of God Everywhere: Poems of the Christian Mystics* (Carlsbad, CA: Hay House, 2009), p. 52.

9. Judy Cannato. *Field of Compassion: How the New Cosmology Is Transforming Spiritual Life* (Notre Dame, IN: Sorin, 2010), p. 191.

22

Hope Beyond the Death of Hope

Though at times it may seem
as if the world has gone mad—
as the dreams of separation
play out within the collective,
things are not always as they seem.
You are the vessel
through which love can come alive here.
Without you, it will not be possible.

—MATT LICATA[1]

Jesus' crucifixion put to death his followers' hopes—their hopes that circumstances would improve, that right governance would be restored, and that justice would finally prevail. We can only imagine their depths of despondency and hopelessness. But just when things seemed their darkest, Jesus rose from the dead. The resurrection brought a far wider vision of hope—a hope that reaches beyond our immediate life circumstances or political situations, a hope that is beyond the death of hope.

In today's world, we see the death of hope in many places. As I write this, my home country of South Africa faces the possibility of economic ruin, which will impact most heavily on those who already live in poverty. Globally, we have gone through years of pandemic, and now we face a time of political upheaval as democracy itself proves to be manipulable and deeply flawed. A collective despair hangs over the Earth, and people are disillusioned as they recognize the mass scale of selfish, greedy, and unethical leadership. Environmentally, we are heading toward disaster at an ever-increasing pace, and we seem to lack the collective will to make any real changes to our lifestyles. Around the world, racism and other forms of prejudice raise their ugly heads. As religious and political liberals and conservatives pit themselves against each other, the separations between us grow and spread. Our hopes for a healthy, unified, and peaceful world have fallen into pieces.

We have to admit that our concerns essentially revolve around ourselves: we worry about the impact all this turmoil will have on the way of life we have become used to (and don't want to let go of). The self-interest of our leaders merely mirrors our own selfishness and greed. When we face this reality honestly, we despair at the plight of humanity.

In a time when we collectively face the death of so many hopes, what does the hope of the resurrection mean? What does *hope beyond the death of hope* mean?

A Radical Invitation to Inner Transformation

The Bible invites us to have the same mindset as Jesus:

> Who, being in very nature God, did not consider equality with God something to be held onto; instead, he made himself nothing by taking the very nature of a servant, being made in human likeness. And being found in appearance as a human, he humbled himself by becoming obedient to death—even death on a cross! (Philippians 2:5–8)

Having the mindset of Jesus means we are willing to follow his example of self-surrender, even to the point of death. This is an invitation to radical inner transformation, a transformation that puts to death our separate senses of self. We surrender our self-interest and self-protection, and we accept the complete dissolution of our false selves, so that we can experience broader, freer, and more loving identities.

Cynthia Bourgeault said that this is the foundation of "the hope that can never be taken away," because you simply know your abiding union in this place of interconnection; you know that nothing can possibly fall out of God. Only from the level of spiritual awareness do you begin to see and trust that all is held in the divine Mercy. But once grounded in that certainty, you can begin to reach out to the world with the same wonderful, generous vulnerability that we see in Christ.[2]

Some people have described this as the next step in the evolution of human consciousness—an all-pervasive awakening from our identities as separate self-interested beings, so that we enter the new creation with all its unexplored possibilities. This can't happen, though, without the ancient pattern of death and resurrection, like the seed that disintegrates in the ground to allow for a larger new life to emerge. This is what Paul meant when he wrote, "I have been crucified with Christ and I no longer live, but Christ lives in me" (Galatians 2:20).

Judy Cannato described this as a "cosmic change" that "will mean the upheaval of our cherished customs and the disposal of stories that have provided the basic framework for our lives."[3] A radical shift in identity like this does not happen by the flick of a wand; it takes time. Although God's grace initiates and sustains the process, it requires our participation. This is why engaging regularly in contemplative practices is so important. We need to make space for God's will, through our ongoing choices to let go of our own wills, so we can flow with the movement of God's Spirit in our lives.

Dying to self—or self-dissolution—involves a habitual choice to clear our self-interest out of the way, like cleaning a lens, so that the pure and uninhibited light of God can shine through. When we wear glasses with lenses filmed with grime, we may not notice how much they are clouding our vision until we take them off and look at them; in a similar way, we often don't realize how much our selfishness obstructs the light and love of God. Just as glasses do not stay clean all by themselves and must be polished frequently, we need regular and intentional practice to wipe away the self-interest that so easily smears our perspectives.

By continually making the choice to let go of the small, selfish self, we allow the Spirit of Truth to reveal where we are still clinging to our old perspectives. As we follow Jesus on his path of descent into death, we are gradually freed from our identification with the tight shell of the false self.

And from this death, new life emerges. We too experience a resurrection, one that offers us hope and life beyond what we can imagine.

Communal Hope

Our individual awakening processes not only benefit us and those who know us; they can also help humanity and the planet. Our species is at a crucial impasse—but as we participate with the death and resurrection of Jesus, on a broader scale, we bring hope beyond the death of hope.

We are all interconnected. "Pick a flower on earth and you move the farthest star," is a statement attributed to physicist Paul Dirac. Along the same lines, the naturalist John Muir stated, "When we try to pick out anything by itself, we find it hitched to everything else in the universe."[4]

To understand this concept a little more deeply, think for a moment about a magnet. Around a magnet lies a region of space that's influenced by the magnet's presence; any magnetic material that comes into this space—which is called the magnetic field—experiences a force. The presence of the magnet alters the space around it, creating a field of far-reaching influence. Although this field is invisible, we can observe it if we place a magnet on a piece of paper and then sprinkle iron filings over the paper; as the iron filings align with the magnetic field, they create a pattern on the paper.

Anything made of iron that enters the magnetic field will experience the magnet's force, even if it is not touching the magnet. If the object is left in the presence of this field long enough, it too becomes magnetized. Furthermore, magnetic fields cooperate with one another in a process called *superposition*, where the fields of nearby magnets add together to create a stronger field.

The gravitational field around the Earth is similar to the field around a magnet; we experience a force of attraction toward the Earth, even when we are not touching it. Some scientists have postulated that similar fields may exist in biology, where these fields help to determine and shape the organization of living cells (just as the magnet shaped the organization of the metal filings sprinkled on the paper). This phenomenon has been named *morphogenic fields*.[5]

The concept has been expanded even further to explain some of the more mysterious ways in which communities learn, behave, and change. *Morphic resonance* is the term that describes the interaction of human knowledge and awareness with one another in a way that is similar to the superposition of magnetic fields. The more morphogenic fields that interact with each other, the more powerful the resonance they create.

Judy Cannato described these invisible regions in communities as "fields of information." She wrote that over time, "morphogenic fields begin to have a cumulative memory and become increasingly habitual, making it easier for those entering the field to learn its associated habits."[6] This, she explained, is why young people are more capable of becoming computer literate than older people, in a much shorter space of time: a "field of knowing" among young people as a group facilitates their learning of computer skills.

If we apply the concept of morphogenic fields to spirituality, we find hope for collective human transformation. Each person who undergoes inner transformation influences the space around them. The greater the number of people who undergo inner transformation, the more the space is altered, allowing others to more readily also enter the transformational process. At some stage, a tipping point may be reached that will cause humanity to collectively transform into a new way of being.

More and more spiritual teachers are describing the process of spiritual transformation as the evolution of human consciousness, from the old individualistic consciousness to a more inclusive, non-dualistic, openhearted, and compassionate consciousness—what in Christian terms is described as *Christ-consciousness*.

Teilhard de Chardin, who saw this as a continuation of the unfolding process of evolution, said:

> Move ever upward toward greater consciousness and greater love! At the summit you will find yourselves united with all those who, from every direction, have made the same ascent. For everything that rises must converge.[7]

Judy Cannato went so far as to claim that the "freedom at the heart of the gospel" is "the capacity to choose to engage in the process of the evolution of consciousness." She went on to say, "We have the capacity to cooperate with the unfolding of the universe, a process driven by grace, which invites us to be co-creators."[8]

In other words, the survival of our entire Earth community depends on each of us awakening from our small, self-interested identities. This is what Paul described when he wrote, "For the creation waits in eager anticipation for the children of God to be revealed" (Romans 8:19).

Through our contemplative practice, we are over and over letting go of our selfishness, surrendering to the mystery of the presence and action of God in us. This self-dissolution process is the only way we can become channels for God's love; our own notions of love are far too small and self-interested. Our human capacity can never achieve self-dissolution on its own, for the process is outside our ability to control, describe, or even understand.

Then, as we participate together in this morphogenic field of self-dissolution and awakening, we take part in the emergence of what Paul described as "the new creation" (2 Corinthians 5:17). This new way of being expresses itself in selfless love, true compassion, and the ability to cooperate beyond our ego boundaries—for the good of all humanity and the planet.

And so, may we have the courage to follow Jesus on his path of descent, servanthood, and apparent nothingness, so that we may be united with him in his resurrection. Together, as we go ever-deeper in the spiritual dimension, may we reveal the doorway into the mystery of God's hope that is beyond the death of hope.

The day will come when,
after harnessing space, the winds,
the tides, and gravitation,
we shall harness for God the energies of love.
And on that day, for the second time
in the history of the world,
we shall have discovered fire.

—TEILHARD DE CHARDIN[9]

INVITATION TO REFLECT

Spend a while sitting still and focusing gently on your breathing, allowing yourself to become quiet inside. Then answer these questions (you may want to use your journal to do this):

- How do you react to the idea of the total dissolution of your self? Does it feel like a threat—or a hopeful possibility?

- After reading this chapter, do you feel God calling you toward any action or change?

- Now that you have read this final chapter, as you reflect back on the entire book, what concept stands out most? Can you see this as an invitation to enter into a deeper relationship with God?

After you have prayerfully written your responses to these questions, respond to God in whatever way feels most expressive for you.

Now allow yourself to become quiet again, remaining still, open, and receptive to God for a few minutes.

NOTES

1. Matt Licata. From his blog *A Loving Healing Space*, April 15, 2017.

2. Cynthia Bourgeault. *Centering Prayer and Inner Awakening* (Cambridge, MA: Cowley, 2004), p. 17

3. Judy Cannato. *Field of Compassion: How the New Cosmology Is Transforming Spiritual Life* (Notre Dame, IN: Ave Maria, 2010), p. 182.

4. John Muir. *My First Summer in the Sierra* (Oakland, CA: Sierra Club Books, 1988), p. 110.

5. Rupert Sheldrake is the scientist whose name is most often attached to this idea. Although many in the scientific community believe Sheldrake's ideas to be incorrect, even laughably so, other credible scientists have cited research that supports Sheldrake (for example, see "Morphogenic Fields: A Coming of Age" by K. E. Thorpe, published in the March-April 2022 edition of *EXPLORE: The Journal of Science & Healing*, https://www.sciencedirect.com). You can read more about Sheldrake's theory in his online article "Morphic Resonance and Morphic Fields: An Introduction" at https://www.sheldrake.org/research/morphic-resonance/introduction.

6. Cannato, p. 30.

7. In an interview with *EnlightenNext Magazine* (November 3, 2010), spiritual anthropologist Jean Houston described her chance meetings with Pierre Teilhard de Chardin when she was fourteen. She took notes on some of the things he said to her (though at the time she did not know who he was), which included these sentences, the last he said to her before he died. Earlier, he had told her, "We are being called into metamorphosis, into a far higher order, and yet we often act only from a tiny portion of ourselves. It is necessary that we increase that portion. But do not think for one minute, Jean, that we are alone in making that possible. We are part of a cosmic evolutionary movement that inspires us to unite with God. This is the lightning flash for all our potentialities. This is the great originating cause of all our shifts and changes."

8. Cannato, p. 37.

9. Pierre Teilhard de Chardin. *Toward the Future*, René Hague, trans. (New York: Harcourt Brace Jovanovich, 1975), pp. 86–87.

PERMISSIONS

AUTHOR BIO

SHARON GRUSSENDORFF has a PhD in quantum computational physics and lectured at the University of KwaZulu-Natal in South Africa for ten years. She has since worked for the past twenty years as a consultant for science education development, project management, editing, and research. She also leads the Dove Fellowship, which is a church in Pietermaritzburg, South Africa, with a contemplative focus, and she is the co-founder and spiritual director at the Solitude Retreat Centre in the KwaZulu-Natal Midlands. She completed a two-year training with the Living School for Action and Contemplation, where her teachers were Richard Rohr, Cynthia Bourgeault, and James Finley. She has been facilitating retreats and offering spiritual direction for the past twenty-five years and has spoken at a range of workshops and conferences on contemplation and spiritual well-being.

SITTING WITH GOD
A Journey to Your True Self Through Centering Prayer

"Lewis presents an intimate view of his centering prayer journey. He helps us discover the contemplative life and who we are in the deepest sense, made in God's image."

— Fr. Carl Arico, founding member of Contemplative Outreach Ltd., and author of *A Taste of Silence*

"This work offers a friendly and accessible approach to centering prayer that will be of great benefit to those new to the practice. Rich has a lovely way of inviting the reader in through honest reflections on his own experience, both struggles and graces. These stories offer comfort and gentle encouragement on the way."

— Christine Valters Paintner, author of *The Soul of a Pilgrim*

"Rich Lewis's writing is unique in its simplicity and lack of pretense. And he is nothing if not honest, especially regarding his passion for centering prayer. In this book you will find down-to-earth spiritual practice that echoes throughout Rich's life as a husband, dad, and financial consultant. Highly recommended!"

— Amos Smith, author of *Be Still and Listen*

DANTE'S ROAD
The Journey Home for the Modern Soul

Nautilus Book Awards 2019 Gold Winner

This spiritual guidebook follows in the footsteps of Dante on his journey through the *Divine Comedy*. A fresh, modern take on this path, the book invites us to explore these questions: what is my hell and how do I move through it? What is my purgatory and what lesson do I need to take away? What is my paradise; how do I get there and how do I stay there? With wisdom distilled from the great myths, scriptures, and the world's mystics, this book is an invitation to ever-greater awakening and wholeness.

"We're lost. We're trying to get home. With those words, Marc Thomas Shaw aptly summarizes the human predicament and then gathers a host of wise counselors—from mythology, pop culture, spiritual masters, and his own lived experiences—to accompany the reader on an inner journey toward the soul's true home."

— Kenneth McIntosh, author of *Water from an Ancient Well: Celtic Spirituality for Modern Life*

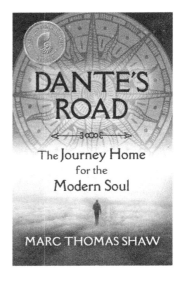

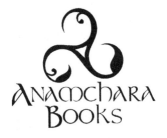

ANAMCHARA
BOOKS

www.AnamcharaBooks.com